Fine WoodWorking
on Things to Make

Fine WoodWorking
on **Things to Make**

35 articles selected by the editors of *Fine Woodworking* magazine

The Taunton Press

Cover photo by Curtis Almquist

First printing: September 1986
International Standard Book Number: 0-918804-51-5
Library of Congress Catalog Card Number: 86-50404
Printed in the United States of America

A FINE WOODWORKING Book

FINE WOODWORKING® is a trademark of The Taunton Press, Inc.,
registered in the U.S. Patent and Trademark Office.

The Taunton Press, Inc.
63 South Main Street
Box 355
Newtown, Connecticut 06470

Contents

Introduction

Most woodworkers I know are compulsive makers. They build things of wood not so much to have the finished product but to satisfy an inner yearning to experiment, to learn and to create. It's a feeling, I imagine, akin to an artist's need to paint or a musician's need to play. Cookbook-style project books full of slavishly dimensioned plans don't appeal to these folks. They much prefer the inspiration of a good idea, say, for a dining table or a comfortable chair, which can be altered to suit, thus providing fertile ground to try a new technique or an interesting detail learned along the way.

This volume is a book of ideas. It contains 35 articles on making all kinds of wooden objects from practical, everyday furniture to toys to fanciful musical instruments. These articles, drawn from the first ten years of *Fine Woodworking* magazine, are also rich in woodworking techniques that you'll find invaluable in building projects of your own design.

Paul Bertorelli, editor

Starting Out
Edge-joining for the beginner

by Roger Holmes

While practicing basic woodworking skills, you can make this simple dining table and bookcase, or variations to suit your fancy.

A friend of mine took a beginners' woodworking course not too long ago. She was surprised, and a little disappointed, to discover that the first two sessions were devoted not to the construction of a coffee table or a dovetailed box but to the making of a simple, ordinary board—two flat, parallel faces, and square to them, two straight edges.

Board-making is not exactly the stuff of woodworking romance. But without boards it's tough to make tables and cabinets. In this article I'll tackle board-making; in subsequent articles, I'll cover other basics—cutting bridle joints, rabbets, and so on. My methods aren't definitive, but I hope they'll get you going.

Making sample joints isn't much fun, so if you don't have your own projects to practice on, you can cobble up the table and bookcase shown above as you go along. (Make the 48-in. dia. tabletop now, the table base with the next article, the bookcase with the third and fourth.) I built these pieces after my wife and I moved our meager possessions into a seven-room apartment and needed to fill up the empty spaces. The results are hardly masterpieces of design or construction, but you can generate a lot of simple furniture from them. Chests of drawers, after all, are just little boxes housed in a big box; tables, merely slabs of wood perched at various heights above the floor.

Wood—I decided to build the table and bookcase of solid wood, even though using plywood would have eliminated gluing up wide boards. I enjoy working solid wood. Curling a long shaving out of my plane gives me a great deal of satisfaction—planing plywood produces grit and dust.

There is solid wood and solid wood, however. Some woods, such as rosewood and walnut, seem to demand elegant designs. But what I wanted was utility, economy, and something easy and pleasing to work. Pine filled the bill on all counts, and I discovered a small lumberyard up the road selling it for $.30 to $1.00 a board foot (1984 prices).

I strongly recommend that beginners work with pine or a similarly soft, evenly grained wood such as basswood or certain varieties of fir. Mistakes are inevitable and instructive, so you might as well make them cheaply. In lumberman's lingo, you'll need 4/4 (1-in.) boards for the boxes and 8/4 (2-in.) boards for the table.

If you can, buy roughsawn (unplaned) boards. If not, buy the planed, or surfaced, boards sold at most lumberyards. The most common variety of surfaced board is designated S4S, which stands for "surfaced four sides," meaning that the boards have been surfaced on both faces and both edges. No. 2 Common pine boards are fine. They're relatively cheap,

and the knots in them will add character to your furniture (that's as good a rationalization as any for penny-pinching.) Because the boards have been surfaced, they will not be the full nominal thickness. For example, if you want boards between ¾ in. and 1 in. thick after you've flattened them, start with 5/4 S4S stock.

Flattening boards—The tabletop and the box that forms the bookcase base require large, flat expanses of wood. Roughsawn boards from the sawmill or surfaced boards from the lumberyard are seldom flat enough or wide enough. Their faces usually will be cupped across the grain, bowed, or twisted diagonally along the grain, or a combination of all these. Making wide boards by edge-joining requires flat boards, so your first task is to make them that way.

Cabinetmaking, like mathematics, proceeds logically from start to finish. Each step builds on the last, and if you miss something at the beginning, you'll likely suffer for it at the end—or sooner. If the first face isn't reasonably flat, everything that follows will be affected. The sequence is simple: After flattening one face, flatten the other while removing enough wood to bring the board to the right thickness. Then plane the edges square to the faces, and you're ready to glue up.

I think that the hand plane is the most effective tool for flattening. Its mechanical cousin, the jointer, is quicker, but the width of the jointer bed limits the width of board that can be flattened. A thickness planer can make a board uniformly thick, but it can flatten only the thickest boards. Whenever possible, I use a combination of hand and machine techniques. But even if you're blessed with a wide jointer and a planer, it helps to know how to flatten, thickness and joint the edges of boards by hand. In the process, you'll also

From *Fine Woodworking* magazine (September 1984) 48:46-51

For a close shave

Planing with a dull tool is a thankless task. I spent much of my first woodworking year struggling with a dull plane blade, and when I finally managed a keen edge, it was a revelation. It's inevitable that, for a while, you'll be keener than your tools.

In sharpening, the end totally justifies the means, and there are dozens of equally effective routes to a sharp edge. The cutting edge of a plane blade is at the intersection of the bevel and the back of the blade. The ideal edge, like the ideal line in geometry, would have length but no thickness. All sharpening methods try to refine the bevel/back intersection to the ideal by removing steel with finer and finer abrasives.

My sharpening tools are simple: a bench grinder with a medium-grit, 6-in. carborundum wheel; an 8-in. long combination India benchstone, one side coarse, one side fine; a 6-in. long soft Arkansas benchstone; and a leather strop, a piece of belt leather impregnated with a fine abrasive such as rottenstone. (The leather alone, or even the palm of your hand, will do for a strop).

The bevel of a new plane iron is ground to about 25° and I maintain this angle, trying not to facet the bevel when grinding. Most grinders have tool rests that can be fixed, or adapted, to support the blade at the bevel angle. You can grind the cutting edge slightly convex in its length or dub off the corners to prevent making ridges in the wood when you're rough-planing. I use one plane for everything, so I grind straight across, and plane the ridges out with a few strokes of a sharp, finely set blade.

After grinding, rub a little light machine oil on the fine face of the India stone and rest the bevel on it. I hold the blade with one hand, tilt it slightly forward (about 5°) and draw it toward me. The motion can be slow or fast, but hold the blade steady—don't rock it from front to back or side to side. Tilting the blade forms a second bevel, which makes the cutting edge a little more durable.

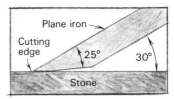

Take six to eight strokes, then feel for a burr of steel rolling over the back of the cutting edge. When the burr appears, move to the soft Arkansas stone and make about as many strokes at the same angle. Then turn the blade over, lay it *flat* on the stone, and rub it back and forth to turn the burr. Alternate on the Arkansas between the bevel and the back until the burr disappears. Then stroke the bevel and back on the leather strop, just as on the stones.

At the end of this little ritual, try to shave the hair off the back of your hand—a clean shave equals a sharp edge. If you tire of being asked about your bald hand, rest the flat side of the blade on your thumbnail, raise it slightly and push the cutting edge toward the cuticle. The lower the angle at which the edge catches on the nail, the sharper it is. If the edge isn't sharp enough, strop again; if that doesn't work, go back to the stones.

That's how I do it. Others hold the blade with both hands, move it in a circle or a figure eight on the stone, strop the edge on their pant leg, and so on. No matter how long it takes, don't get discouraged. Once you get used to it, you can sharpen a plane iron in less time than takes to read about how to do it.   —R.H.

Sharpening on stone

Sharpening involves a series of simple operations, but success requires patience and persistence. Grind a 25° bevel on the blade (below), then refine the edge with increasingly fine benchstones and a leather strop. Try not to rock the blade as you push or pull it across the stones (above). When you move to the soft Arkansas stone, alternate between stroking the bevel and laying the blade *flat* on the stone to turn the burr.

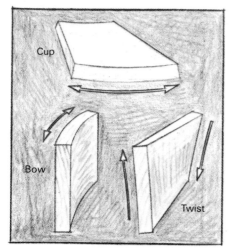

Cup

Bow

Twist

Planing technique

Most boards are afflicted with at least one of the problems shown at left, but can be cured with a hand plane. Hold the plane comfortably; make your whole body work for you. Extend your right index finger along the edge of the blade for added control. Begin with pressure on the plane's toe, and end with pressure on the heel.

acquire dexterity with the plane, which is handy for all sorts of work.

Selecting a plane—Locked up in a London warehouse is my collection of bench planes—eight or nine different sizes, all in working order. When I acquired them, I was teaching myself to woodwork from books and it didn't seem possible to get by with fewer than a half-dozen bench planes. I did my best with them, but the results were mixed. When I went to England to work with master craftsman Alan Peters, I packed them all, eagerly expecting Alan to reveal their secrets. The secret, he told me, was to leave them in the box and use a jointer plane.

I use a 22-in. long, 7½-lb. Stanley-Bailey #07 jointer for everything, from flattening rough lumber to slicing a few thousandths of an inch off the end grain of a 2-in. wide drawer side. The plane is at least 30 years old and cost me $35 used.

I like the jointer's size, weight and balance. Its length and width make it ideal for flattening boards and jointing long edges. It rides over low spots while slicing

Using winding sticks

You can check for twist by sighting across two identical pieces of wood called winding sticks. Get the edges at one end of each stick in your line of sight, then move your eye down the length of the edges. If the edges at the other ends don't line up, the board is twisted. Mark the high corner and the corner diagonal to it; these will have to be planed down.

off the high until everything is flat. And it's heavy enough to maintain solid contact with the wood so most of the pushing can be in the direction of the stroke.

Most important for me is the jointer's balance. Held only by its handle, a jointer remains nearly horizontal—there's about as much weight behind the handle as in front. Balance makes the plane easier to control and less tiring to use.

Every woodworker has a favorite plane. The right bench plane for a job is the one you're most comfortable with—don't be afraid to go against the book and try a plane outside its prescribed territory.

Planing—First determine where the board isn't flat. This can be done by eye, alone or aided by a straightedge, or by feel on a large, flat surface, such as a benchtop, the top of a tablesaw, or the kitchen floor (unless your kitchen floor is like mine and

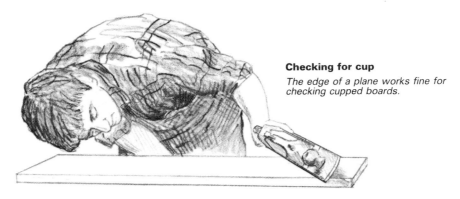

requires sea legs to navigate). Sight across the width of the board to check for cupping and along its length to check for bowing. If you've got a flat surface, check for twist by placing the face of the board on it, then tap each corner in turn. A twisted board will rock, supported on diagonal corners. If you haven't got a flat surface, you can use winding sticks to determine twist, as shown on the facing page.

When you've found and marked the high spots, plane them off. The first problem here is holding the board while you plane. A bench with a tail vise and benchdogs is ideal: pinched between the vise and a stop, most if not all of the board is supported by the benchtop. Lacking a built-in, wooden tail vise, you can mount a regular bench vise on the end of a bench, and bore holes in the benchtop for homemade wooden dogs—¾-in. dia. dowels with scrapwood heads work fine. An easier solution is to drive three or four nails into the benchtop in an L-shaped configuration and shove the board against them. As long as you plane toward the nails, the board won't move.

I set the plane blade to remove as much wood as possible, while still allowing for a comfortable stroke. Position the chip breaker about 1/16 in. back from the cutting edge and make sure that the edge is parallel to the sole of the plane. (Keep the sole and cutting edge parallel for all planing.) I lower the cutting edge as I make the first few strokes. The amount varies with the character of the board, how keen the cutting edge is, and how keen I am to shove away. If you're a hearty soul and the wood is cooperative, you can peel off a goodly shaving (maybe 1/32 in. thick) with each pass. Less blade, less brawn and more strokes will get the job done just as well. If you keep lowering the blade and still slice off only a wisp of wood, or none at all, chances are the blade is dull—take the time to sharpen it.

I hold and push the plane as shown on the facing page. Planing is repetitive work and is most accurately and efficiently done rhythmically, each stroke the same, or nearly the same, as the last. I like to power the stroke with my back and shoulders as well as my arms, shifting weight from front to rear

foot as the stroke progresses. Using your whole body allows you to control the plane with your hands and wrists.

I plane the concave side of a cupped or bowed board first. The plane can too easily follow the contour of the convex side, and you'd just keep planing the same curve rather than flattening it. Regardless of whether the board is cupped, bowed or twisted, it's best to plane diagonally across the board's width, because the plane is less likely to follow and maintain the contour of a long curve or to tear the grain severely. Concentrate on removing the high spots. Check your progress every now and then with a straightedge, flat surface or winding sticks. If the plane is long enough, you can use it as a straightedge, as shown above. A torn and rough surface indicates that you're planing against the grain—try planing the other way. After the face is planed, draw an arrow on it to mark the best direction for planing—the arrow will help you lay out the boards when you're ready to joint the edges.

If the planed board is wide enough to use without gluing up (a bookcase side, for example), smooth any torn grain with

Scribing the thickness
After flattening one face, scribe a line indicating the board's thickness around the edges and ends with a marking gauge. Push the gauge's fence flush to the flat face and its scribe point into the wood. Push or pull the gauge, whichever suits you.

a sharp plane, stroking parallel to the grain direction. Often I make these last strokes after assembling the piece. I don't sand the surfaces, because I like the look and feel of a planed surface—and sanding is no fun at all.

Flattening boards is a good way to get a feel for planing. In the old days, apprentices spent months at it, paying their dues, building up their skill and their biceps. You make lots of strokes, but there isn't a lot of risk involved. About the worst you can do is end up with thinner boards than you wanted. And if you really screw one up, try another—after all, it's just pine.

Thicknessing—When you're satisfied with the first face, you can gauge from it to flatten the second face and thickness the board. Set a marking gauge to the thickness you want (or the thickness you can get—the thinnest spot on the edges or ends), then run it around the edges and ends of the board. Now plane down to the scribe, just as for flattening.

If you don't want to thickness boards by hand, a local millwork shop might do it for you by machine. If you haven't flattened one side, make sure they do, otherwise you'll just end up with uniformly thick boards that are still cupped, bowed or twisted. Also let them know beforehand if the boards are pine—some shops won't machine resinous woods.

Edge-jointing—When you've got a stack of flat boards, a pile of fragrant shavings and a pair of sore arms, you're ready to plane the edges for gluing up. This is less strenuous than flattening or thicknessing, but more exacting. I've come to appreciate bookcases that can be made without edge-joined boards. Tabletops and deeper boxes, unfortunately, can seldom be made without gluing up boards. Once I'm resigned to necessity, I usually enjoy the technical challenge of making good edge joints.

The ideal edge joint consists of two edges, planed straight, flat and square to their adjacent faces, cemented together with a microscopic layer of glue. In practice, the edges needn't be square or flat as

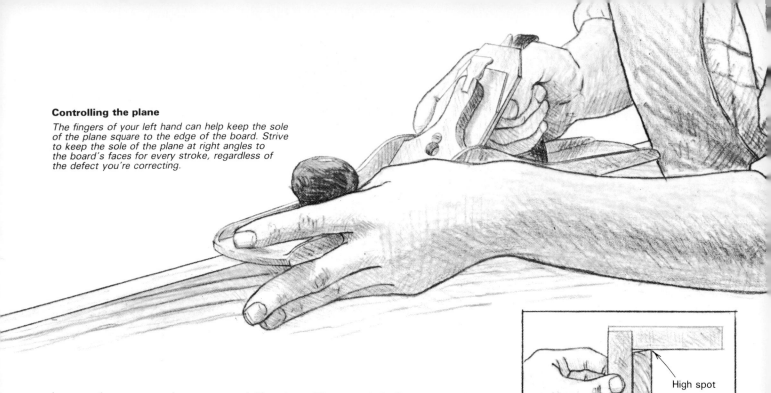

Controlling the plane

The fingers of your left hand can help keep the sole of the plane square to the edge of the board. Strive to keep the sole of the plane at right angles to the board's faces for every stroke, regardless of the defect you're correcting.

High spot

Checking the edges

Check the squareness of an edge with a try square. Sight into a light source as you slide the square along the edge. Light between the edge and the blade indicates a high spot. If high spots at each end are on diagonally opposed corners, the edge is twisted. Check mating edges with a straightedge, as shown below. If the surface isn't fairly flat, adjust the angle of one or both edges to the faces.

long as they are complementary, and if the edges are slightly concave in their length, the joints will be less prone to open at the ends. That said, I still *try* to plane edges flat and square.

Lay out the boards for the tabletop or box side on a flat surface. Arrange them so the grain pattern and colors please you. If you have a slightly bowed board, place it between straight ones—it can be pulled into alignment when you clamp up. Run all the grain-direction arrows you made earlier in the same direction, so you'll be less likely to tear the surface when planing it flat after glue-up. Finally, mark the relative positions of the boards by drawing a large V across their faces—reconstituting the V will restore the order.

Sharpen the plane blade before edge-jointing, and set the chip breaker within $\frac{1}{32}$ in. or less of the cutting edge. Make sure the cutting edge is parallel to the sole, then adjust the iron during the first few strokes to take a heavy shaving for roughing out the edge, or a fine one for finishing.

Put the first board edge-up in a bench vise. (Long boards narrower than 2 in. to 3 in. should be planed edge-up on the benchtop between dogs or against a nail, so they won't bend under the pressure of planing.) Sight down the length of the edge to determine if it's convex or con-

Edge-planing

Edge-planing strokes should be slower and more controlled, but no less rhythmic, than flattening strokes. Power the plane with your body; orient it with your hands. Put pressure on the toe at the start, and on the heel at the finish of a stroke.

cave. Check the edge for squareness to the faces with a try square. You can sight down the edge as you slide the square along it, marking high spots as you go.

The secret to edge-planing is to always hold the plane with its sole perpendicular to the faces of the board. I extend three fingers of my left hand over the edge of the plane, where they rub against the wood, forming a fence and giving a surprisingly accurate sense of the angle of plane to face. Use your whole body to power the plane; control it with your hands. Get the edge roughly in shape with rapid strokes, but finish evenly and deliberately. (When there's a machine jointer handy, I rough out the edges on it and finish them with the hand plane to remove the tiny ridges created by the machine.)

Because planing edges is so exacting, its success depends upon all sorts of factors—chiefly, practice. So don't fuss too much with the first edge; when you feel it's straight, flat and square to the faces, plane the mating edge on the next board. Then, while the second board is still in the vise, place the first edge on the second to check the fit. The top board should rest steadily on the bottom one. If it rocks, one or both of the edges is convex and/or twisted.

A concave or convex edge is easy to see; a twisted edge is not so easy. Press down on one end of the top board and look closely at the joint at the other end. If an edge is twisted, the surfaces will touch only at one corner; if they don't touch at all, the edge is convex. (Edges may, of course, be convex and twisted at the same time—I try to correct the convexity first.) You can also check for twist with a try square. If there are diagonally opposed high spots at the ends, the edge is twisted.

It doesn't hurt if the edges are slightly concave—but not more than $\frac{1}{32}$ in. over 3 ft. To fix an excessively concave edge, take a few strokes off each end and one the full length, then recheck. To flatten a convex edge, work out from the center, taking three or four progressively longer strokes, finishing with a full-length stroke.

A twisted edge requires a more delicate fix. As when flattening a twisted face, you want to plane from corner to corner to remove the diagonally opposed high spots. If the sole of the plane is perpendicular to the board's faces, you should be able to take a shaving from just the high spot at the near end, reach a full-width shaving in the center of the edge, and nip off the other high spot at the opposite end. When you think the twist is gone, take a full-width shaving from end to end, and

check against the mating edge. If the boards still rock, the mating edge may need work. This can go on for some time. Don't lose heart—think of all the skill you're accumulating.

Twisted edges need to be fixed, but it doesn't matter if mating edges are at slightly other than right angles to their adjacent faces—as long as the angles are complementary, the boards will form a flat surface. To check the surface, stack the boards edge-to-edge and place a straightedge against their faces. If the surface isn't flat, adjust the angle of one edge to its face and check them again. After edge-planing all the boards to be glued together, stack them up and make a final check for flatness.

Hand-planing mating edges is a difficult skill to master. Over and over again you'll introduce one fault while trying to correct another. When the edges are close to mating perfectly, force yourself to try one more time to correct that last niggling fault. If it still isn't right, then say the hell with it, and move on to the next pair. Among the virtues of modern glues is their ability to join edges that are far from perfectly matched. There may be gaps, the joined boards may not be perfectly flat, but they will stick together. The simple table and bookcase are nice projects because you get a lot of practice while making something useful. It's up to you how much practice you can stand before you need to see the completed piece before you.

Gluing up—When all the pairs of mating edges have been planed, I glue up with $\frac{3}{4}$-in. pipe clamps and Elmer's Glue-All (a white glue), first making a dry run to de-

termine the position and number of clamps. Place clamps 12 in. to 15 in. apart, starting and ending about 3 in. from the ends of the boards. Alternate the clamps top and bottom to equalize their pull and avoid cupping the glued-up boards.

Lay the bottom clamps on a flat surface and spread glue on all the edges to be joined. Better too much glue than too little—the excess will get squeezed out of a tight joint anyway. Place the boards on the clamps and rub the mating edges together until glue squeezes out. Draw the joints together with the center clamp, then work out toward each end. I align the faces of the boards with a 16-oz. hammer and a hardwood block, driving them down on the clamps, which helps keep the boards from cupping or twisting as a unit.

It's important that the surface of the glued-up boards lie in a single plane while the glue cures. Whether the boards lie flat or lean against a wall, you can sight over the clamps just like over winding sticks, and shim up low corners to align them.

The glued-up boards can be treated like a single board now, and cleaned off with a sharp plane. Chances are the surface will be slightly cupped, but I don't worry too much about that. The understructure of a table or the corner joints of a box can pull it fairly flat. At this point, the whole question of flatness boils down to what irritates you more: a gently rolling tabletop with wobbling plates and teacups, or seemingly endless tabletop planing. □

Roger Holmes is an associate editor at Fine Woodworking.

Starting Out
Cutting a bridle joint

by Roger Holmes

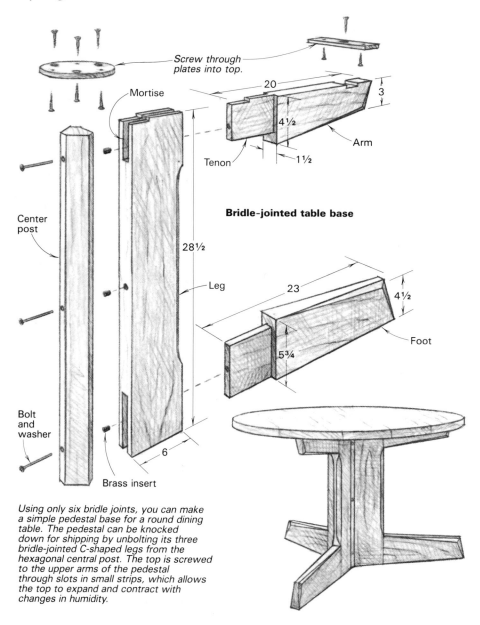

Screw through plates into top.

Mortise

Tenon

20

4½

1½

3

Arm

Bridle-jointed table base

Center post

28½

Leg

23

4½

5¾

Foot

Bolt and washer

6

Brass insert

Using only six bridle joints, you can make a simple pedestal base for a round dining table. The pedestal can be knocked down for shipping by unbolting its three bridle-jointed C-shaped legs from the hexagonal central post. The top is screwed to the upper arms of the pedestal through slots in small strips, which allows the top to expand and contract with changes in humidity.

The mortise-and-tenon is one of the most basic and versatile of all woodworking joints. It can be as plain as the rung-to-leg joints used in any stick chair, or as complicated as some of the three-dimensional, jigsaw-puzzle joints used in Japanese house carpentry. A mortise-and-tenon can be used almost any time you need to join the end of one piece to the edge of another. They're such effective joints that it's hard to find a piece of furniture without at

least one, even if only a dowel in a hole.

The bridle joint (shown above) is one of the simplest garden-variety mortise-and-tenons. Its open-ended mortise doesn't have the mechanical (unglued) strength of an enclosed mortise, but modern glues and the joint's ample gluing surface make up the difference. And a bridle joint can be made more quickly and easily. Both tenon and mortise can be cut almost entirely with a saw, eliminating the excavation that would be required to

clear out an enclosed mortise (see p. 13).

When I was figuring out the base for the round pine dining table shown here, bridle joints seemed ideal. A pedestal eliminates obstruction under the table, and the C-shaped, bridle-jointed frames are sturdy enough to support the table-top, Thanksgiving turkey and a dozen or so elbows. And the six bridle joints are all the joinery needed for the entire base. (See the first article in this series, on pages 2-7, for how to join boards for a top.)

I cut the bridle joints with a bandsaw and backsaw, then used a chisel and shoulder plane to clean up and fit them together. If you don't have a bandsaw, you can do all the sawing with a backsaw and a bowsaw or handsaw (see p. 10). A shoulder plane is handy, but if you're reluctant to dish out $40 or so (1984 prices), you can trim the shoulders with a chisel.

When I knew roughly what sort of table I wanted, I designed it on the workshop floor with a piece of chalk. I drew an elevation (side view) of half the top and one frame full-scale, then fiddled with the proportions until they looked good. If you start with the drawing shown here, sketching a full-scale elevation will help fix the project in your mind. You can change the dimensions and shapes, but I think you'll find the table too shaky if you make the arms, legs or feet much less than 4 in. wide or 1¼ in. thick. The feet will get in the way if they extend beyond the top's circumference. I made the top 4 ft. in diameter, but I think the table would look better with a 5-ft. top.

When your plans are chalked out, cut three sets of arms, legs and feet for the C-shaped frames. Cut all the parts to width and length, but don't shape them yet—it's a lot easier to cut joints in rectangular stock. Next plane the parts flat and to thickness—mine were 1½ in. thick. Try to make them all the same thickness, but don't get bogged down if there's ¹⁄₁₆ in. or so variance—the parts can be planed flush after the frames are glued up. Mark the flattest face of each piece, plane the edges straight and square to it, then mark the most accurate edge (I use a little squiggle on the good face, joined to a V on the good edge). The tolerances needn't be up to edge-joining standards, but the closer the better. Don't worry about making the ends exactly square; a good sawcut is fine.

Laying out—Like any mortise-and-tenon, bridle joints require accurate, organized marking out. To avoid errors, mark all the joints at once, before cutting. You'll

From *Fine Woodworking* magazine (November 1984) 49:68-73

Marking the shoulders

Knife the tenon shoulder lines around each arm and foot. Hold the square's stock against only the good edge or face as you go.

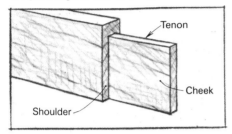

Tenon

Cheek

Shoulder

need to mark wherever a sawcut must be made. As the drawings above and below show, I marked the shoulders with a square and knife, and the cheeks with a mortise gauge, which is just a marking gauge with two pins that scribe both cheeks at once. When laying out each joint, always reference the square and marking gauge from *only* the marked good face and good edge of each part.

For the pedestal, I arranged the parts for each frame on the bench: good-face marks up, good-edge marks to the top of the arm, the bottom of the foot and the inside of the leg. Mark one end of each leg for reference, then identify both parts of each joint with the same number or letter.

Lay out the tenons first. To reduce er-

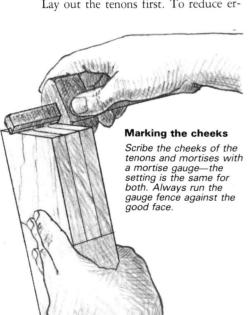

Marking the cheeks

Scribe the cheeks of the tenons and mortises with a mortise gauge—the setting is the same for both. Always run the gauge fence against the good face.

ror, I avoid measuring wherever possible by scribing dimensions directly from the parts being joined. Here, all the tenons are as long as the legs are wide, so I laid one foot across its leg in the position it would be joined, and marked the shoulder position on the edge with a pencil. Using this foot as a guide, I marked the shoulders on the remaining feet and arms. (If the tenons are $\frac{1}{32}$ in. or so shorter than the leg width, clamping will be easier and the surfaces can be planed flush after assembly.)

When you've marked all the tenon lengths, scribe the shoulder lines using a try square and a sharp pocket knife or utility knife. I've devised a little ritual to ensure that I'm scribing only from the good face and edge: First I scribe across the good face, holding the stock of the square against the good edge. Then I scribe across each edge, holding the stock against the good face. Finally I scribe across the second face, holding the stock against the good edge. The lines should connect around the piece. If they don't, the good face is probably twisted. If they come close, don't worry about it--you can take care of the discrepancy when you fit the joint. If they're way off, I'd replane the face, or pick another board and start over.

Lay out the ends of the mortises next. I made the tenons about 1 in. narrower than the full width of the arm and foot—the length of the mortise equals the width of the tenon, so there's less mortise to saw out. Pencil the mortise length on the good faces of the legs, then extend the line across the edges with a try square and knife.

The cheeks of the tenons and the mortises can be scribed with a marking gauge or a mortise gauge. When the mortised and the tenoned pieces are the same thickness, I make tenons about three-fifths that thickness. If the tenon is much thicker, the width of the mortise will make its walls too thin and liable to break. Cutting and cleaning up the mortises will be easier if you make the tenon thickness match a standard auger-bit and chisel size—I made the tenons for the C-shaped frames $\frac{5}{8}$ in. thick.

Set the mortise gauge and

scribe around the edges and ends of the pieces, from shoulder line to shoulder line. When setting up a mortise gauge, I set the distance between the pins, then adjust the fence so that the mortise will be centered on the edge. An easy way to set the fence is to gauge from both faces of the piece, tapping the fence until pin marks made from each face coincide. Scribe all the tenons and mortises with this gauge setting. (At the same time, scribe several offcuts from the frame pieces to use when setting up the bandsaw for cutting the joints.) Make sure you run the fence against the good faces so the

Cutting the cheeks

Bandsaw the tenon cheeks against a straight, squared-up fence. Make sure the sawkerf is in the waste, and try to saw right to the scribe, leaving half of it on the tenon. (After boring the mortises, saw them the same way.)

Saw-blade

Scribe

Waste

possible to glue on a piece of veneer to fill out the tenon's thickness, or you can clamp the slightly flexible walls of the mortise down on the tenon. If the tenon is rattling around in the mortise, cut another one. The extra practice won't do any harm, and if you're using pine, it's cheap enough that you shouldn't flinch as the mistake hits the firewood pile.

Even if the tenon shoulders have been perfectly cut, a pass with a finely set shoulder plane will smooth whatever roughness is left by the saw. Often more doctoring is required to make both shoulders tight to the mortised piece. If the knifed shoulder line is visible, plane down to it, then work by trial and error, assembling the joint and marking the high spots with pencil for removal. To avoid chipping the edge of the piece at the end of the cut, turn the plane around and pull it toward you to complete the cut. I don't usually check the shoulders for squareness as I go along, but when the shoulders are tight, I check the assembled pieces with a framing square. If they don't form a right angle, a couple of shavings off one end of the shoulders usually will fix things.

It doesn't matter how much you plane off the shoulders when making these C-shaped frames; no one will notice if one leg or arm is shorter than another. But if you're making a four-sided frame, such as for a door, you must make the shoulder-to-shoulder lengths of the rails equal, otherwise the frame won't be square.

Finishing up—Before gluing up, I tapered the arms and feet and cut the chamfers. The shape of the frame can be altered as you wish. I played around with various curves for the inside edges before deciding on the simple solution shown in the drawing on p. 8. Layout goes faster if you make cardboard templates, particu- larly if anything is curved. I traced around tapered templates for the arm and foot, bandsawed the waste and planed off the sawmarks. Leave the ends square for clamping, then trim and chamfer them after gluing up.

The first time I made one of these frames, I cut the arm and foot chamfers with a hand plane and the leg chamfers with a spokeshave. The job got done, but it took a long time. Prodded by a friend, I later tried a drawknife. Much to my surprise, it was not the crude implement I had expected, but a tool as capable of taking thin, controlled shavings as of lopping off great chunks of wood. The next set of chamfers took a third as long.

If you drawknife the chamfers, spend some time practicing on scrapwood before slicing into the real thing.

You'll get used to the tool and discover pleasing proportions for your chamfers. The main prerequisite for successful drawknifing is a sharp blade. I sharpen mine like a carving tool: a large bevel on one side and a small bevel on the other. The small bevel helps you control the tool, which is important because a drawknife has no sole to govern its depth of cut. (I hold the blade still and move the stones over it; you may prefer the reverse. For more tips, see "For a close shave" on p. 3.) A slicing cut increases control and produces the cleanest surfaces. You can

Chamfering

A sharp drawknife makes fast, accurate work of chamfering. Work to pencil lines or by eye. Sharpening the blade with two bevels (long on the top, short on the bottom) increases control for fine cuts.

Top bevel

Bottom bevel

chamfer freehand or to penciled guide-lines. If you're after precision, finish with a plane and a spokeshave.

Gluing up the frames is a snap. Squirt glue on the tenon and mortise cheeks and spread it around with a long, thin stick. The glue film needn't be thick; just make sure that all surfaces of the cheeks are covered to ensure a good bond. (If you aren't too quick with the stick or you're gluing up in hot weather, use a white glue, like Elmer's Glue-All, instead of a quick-setting yellow glue, like Titebond.)

Slide the tenons into the mortises, pushing the tenon hard up against the end of the mortise. I pull the shoulders tight with pipe clamps, which doesn't require much pressure, then take these off and clamp across the cheeks with quick-action clamps or C-clamps, using the offcuts from the cheeks for clamping pads. Thicker pads will distribute the pressure better and produce a thinner glueline. A thick glueline might be unsightly on a door, where the edges show, but it doesn't really matter here.

When the glue has cured, plane the faces of the frames flush with a jointer plane—there can be quite a bit to plane off a misaligned joint, but no one will notice if one frame is a little thinner than another. Next trim and chamfer the ends of the arms and feet. The three frames

Gluing up

Cover the mortise and tenon cheeks with glue, then pull the joints together with pipe clamps (that's why you left the ends square). When the shoulders are tight, clamp across the cheeks, using wooden pads to distribute the pressure and protect the surfaces.

should all be the same size, with the outside edges of the arms and feet square to the outside edge of the leg. Stack the frames face to face to find the shortest one, then plane it square if necessary, checking with a framing square. Plane the other two to match, checking each against the first rather than checking with a tape measure and square. It's surprising how discrepancies that can hardly be seen can readily be detected with the fingertips.

I attached each of the frames to a central hexagonal post with three bolts. If you'll never need to disassemble the pedestal, you could glue the frames to the post. I cut the post on the tablesaw, setting the blade at 30° to rip the corners off a 2¾-in. square. The post takes some fussing to fit. I planed three faces 1⅝ in. wide; the others finished narrower.

Bore the bolt holes in the post, offsetting the three holes at each location. Clamp the post to each leg in turn, marking through the holes onto the leg's edge, then bore pilot holes. You could lag-bolt the legs to the post, but the bolts will strip out after too many disassemblies. I used ⁵⁄₁₆-in. dia. machine bolts and brass inserts, which have wood threads on the outside and machine threads on the inside. You can buy the inserts from Wood-craft Supply. If you thread a jamb nut and then the insert onto a hex-head bolt that fits the insert, you can drive it home with a socket and ratchet, then back out the bolt. (This prevents shearing-off of the screwdriver slots under pressure.)

I bandsawed the top round, spoke-shaved the edge smooth (a rasp or file would do, too) and chamfered the arrises with a drawknife. The base is screwed to the top through small wooden strips and a wooden center plate let into the arms. Single screw holes are fine in the center plate, but slotting the holes in the strips will help allow the top to move with changes in humidity.

I don't like the look of varnished pine, so I just paste-waxed the table. This doesn't provide a great deal of protection, so we scrub it down regularly with a potato brush and hot, soapy water. I wouldn't say the table has patina, but it wears its scars well and I don't worry when a guest spills wine or the baby bashes it with his spoon. □

Enclosed mortises

Many mortise-and-tenon joints require an enclosed mortise, rather than the open mortise of the bridle joint. Lay out the mortise using the same marking-gauge setting as for the tenon. I clear the bulk of the waste by boring a series of adjoining holes with a bit the same width as or slightly smaller than the mortise width. Bore about ¹⁄₁₆ in. deeper than the tenon length. Then slice down the cheeks with a wide, sharp chisel, splitting the gauge line. The only tricky part is keeping the chisel straight. Clean up the mortise bottom with a narrow chisel, so the tenon doesn't bottom out.

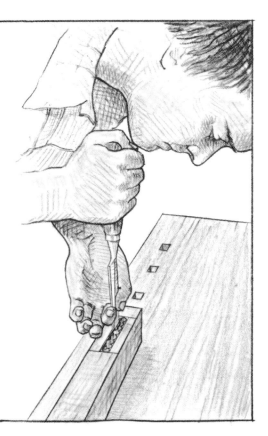

Starting Out
Simple bookcase joints

by Roger Holmes

I can't remember the last time I rented a house with bookshelves (or enough closets for that matter, but I own a lot more books than shirts). So for years I've lived with makeshift shelves—planks on bricks and brackets, planks wedged into alcoves. Confronted with still another shelfless house recently, I finally decided to make some permanent shelves that could move with me from house to house. The result, a stack of two simple boxes, one shallow, one deep, is shown in the drawing at right.

Boxes—called carcases in traditional parlance—are the cabinetmaker's basic building blocks. Stripped down to essentials, most casework isn't much more than a box-like container, usually filled with boxy drawers. In fact, most of the furniture in my house is made of simple rectangular boxes. For example, scale down the shallow box shown on top in the drawing for a spice rack or knickknack shelves; add a mirrored door and you've got a medicine cabinet. Slide a stack of smaller boxes into the deep bottom box and you've got a chest of drawers (I'll show how to do this in a subsequent article).

I made my boxes of pine, tailoring the depth of the upper box to the width of the boards I had on hand. I started with 10-in. wide boards for that box, but tapered the sides to add a little stability and to break the monotony of all those rectangles. The wider sides, top and bottom of the lower box had to be edge-joined and glued up.

Box joinery can be as simple or as complex as your skill and patience permit. Anybody can nail a butt joint together, and for some things that's joint enough. Secret mitered dovetails are at the other end of the scale, and I don't know many people who use them regularly. For my bookshelves, I wanted more strength than

a simple nailed butt joint would give, but I didn't want to spend a lot of time getting it. The upper box, therefore, was put together entirely with dadoes—strong, easily cut joints in which the full thickness of each shelf end is housed in a groove in the side. (If you want adjustable shelves, just dado the top and bottom shelves and support the others on dowels as shown for the adjustable shelf in the lower box.)

Because the lower box had to have a

flush, flat top, the top couldn't be dadoed into the sides. You could nail the ends of the top in rabbets in the sides, but the tongue-and-groove shown in the drawing locks together, which makes the joint stronger and much easier to assemble. The carcase bottom dadoes into the sides. Eighth-inch tempered Masonite backs strengthen both boxes, an important factor if you want adjustable shelves in the upper box. Whether you nail the back

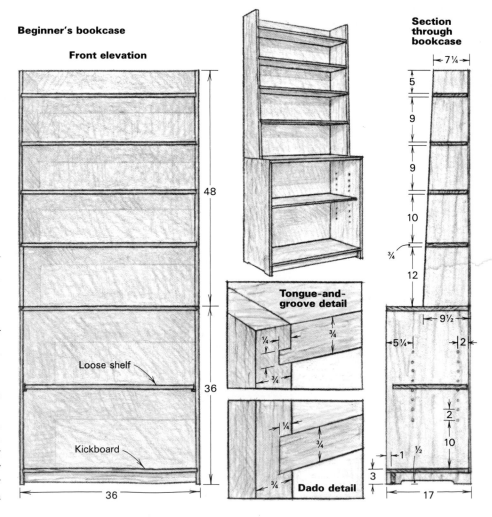

Beginner's bookcase

Front elevation

Loose shelf

Kickboard

48

36

36

Tongue-and-groove detail

¼
¾
¾
¾

Dado detail

¼
¾
¾

Section through bookcase

7¼
5
9
9
10
¾
12
9½
5¼
2
2
10
1
½
3
17

From *Fine Woodworking* magazine (January 1985) 50:54-59

over the back edges or into a rabbet affects only the looks, not the strength. I reinforced all the joints with finishing nails; screws would add even more strength. If the joints fit snugly and the boxes have backs, simply gluing them will be enough.

The carcase joints I've described can be cut by hand or machine. I'll explain the hand methods here, and the router and tablesaw alternatives on pp. 18-19.

First prepare the parts. Flatten, thickness and glue up the boards, either by hand as described in the first article in this series (see pp. 2-7) or with a jointer and thickness planer. Try to make all the parts at least ¾ in. thick. The exact thickness of the shelves of the upper box and the bottom of the lower box depends on the width of the dadoes. I cut a test dado in scrapwood and thicknessed the boards to fit it snugly. Tight joints present a dilemma: The tighter the joints, the stronger the box, but the harder it will be to glue up. You should have to apply some pressure to assemble a joint dry, but you shouldn't have to hammer it home. If anything, make the shelves too thick for now—it's easier to make a board thinner than to shim a loose joint.

Next rip the boards to width and crosscut them to length. (Since the back is let into a rabbet in both boxes, the shelves have to be narrower than the sides, so that their back edge will be flush with the bottom of the rabbet.) Mark the good face and good edge. From now until you cut the joints, the top and bottom of the lower box are worked in the same way as the shelves of the upper box, so I'll just lump them all together and call them shelves.

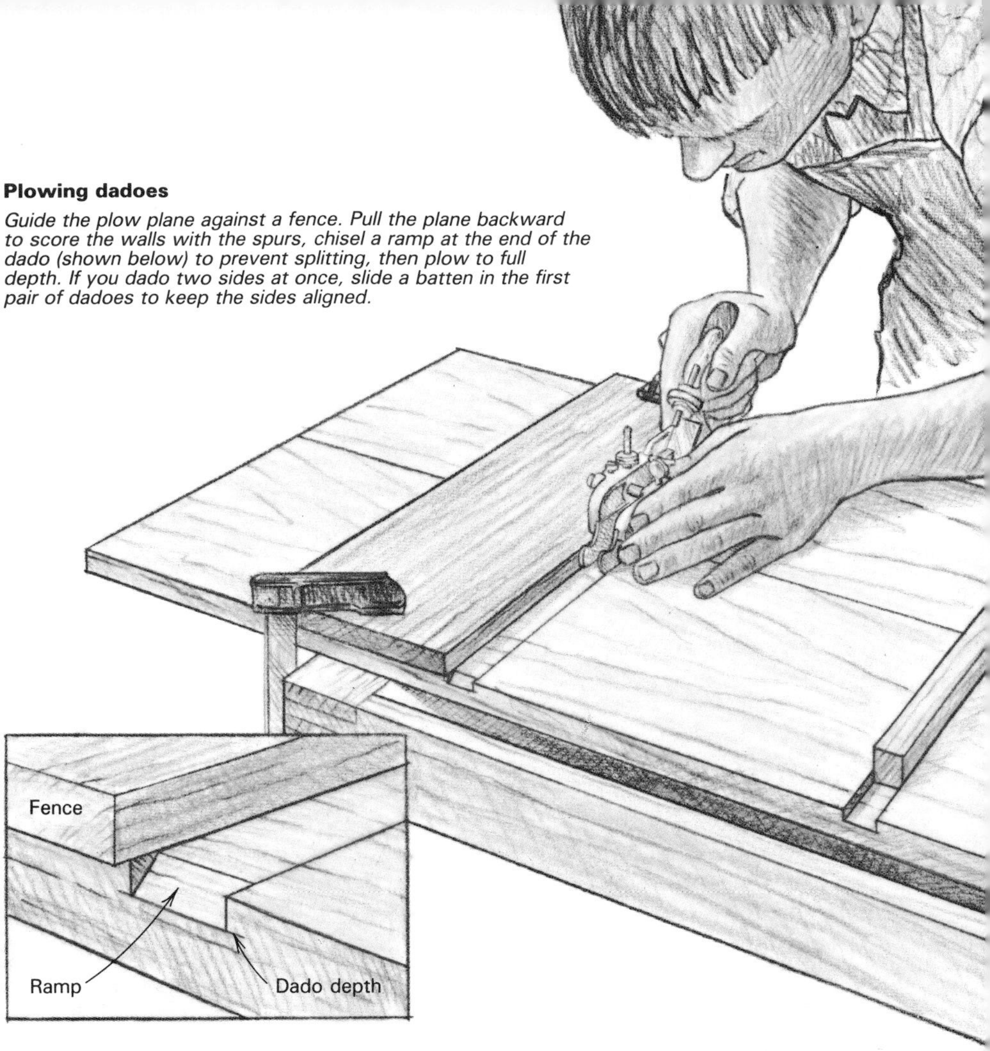

The ends of all the shelves should be square to their edges, and the shelves should all be the same length. Your tablesaw or radial-arm saw may be very accurate, but mine leave the pieces slightly off, so I finish the job with a jointer plane. Stack the shelves so you can pick out the shortest one to square up first.

Planing end grain isn't particularly difficult, and the techniques are similar to those for planing edges (see article on pp. 2-7). Check the end against the good edge with a framing square or a try square, and mark the high corner. Put the board end-up in the face vise. If the board is short enough, position the end only a couple of inches above the bench to cut down on chatter. Adjust the plane to take a thin shaving, then plane in from the high corner—to avoid splintering the edge, don't run the plane off the far corner. Un-

Plowing dadoes

Guide the plow plane against a fence. Pull the plane backward to score the walls with the spurs, chisel a ramp at the end of the dado (shown below) to prevent splitting, then plow to full depth. If you dado two sides at once, slide a batten in the first pair of dadoes to keep the sides aligned.

Fence

Ramp   Dado depth

less your saw is way out of whack, a couple of shavings should square the end to the good edge. The end needn't be dead square to the face, but if it's too far off, the joint won't be as strong. With the shortest shelf square, use it as a template for the rest, stacking it and the next shelf, then feeling with your fingertips for discrepancies in the ends. Square the box sides the same way.

Before I cut any of the dadoes, I pencil in their positions on the sides. Place the good edges of the paired sides together, ends flush, and simultaneously mark the locations of both walls of each dado on the two inside faces to ensure that the shelf spacing is exactly the same on both. Extend these marks across each inside face with a framing square, holding the square against the good edge. Also clearly mark the bottom of the inside face of each side. The spacing shown in the drawing on the facing page accommodates most of my books, but alter it to suit yours.

The depth of the dado isn't critical, but it shouldn't be more than half the side's thickness. A deeper dado would be stronger, but too hard to assemble. One-quarter to one-third the thickness of the side is plenty. Scribe the dado depths on the edges with a marking gauge.

Dadoing by hand is satisfying work if you're not in a hurry. You'll need a plow plane—a straightforward tool that requires a little practice. A simple metal plow plane consists of a handle attached to one of two fairly thin runners that form the body. The handled runner holds the blade and is fitted with two bars on which the other runner slides. The outer faces of the runners are set flush with the edges of the cutter, which can be one of a variety of widths. A fence, which also fits on the bars, can guide the plane along the edge or end of the work. I've had good luck plowing easy-to-work woods like pine or mahogany; harder woods are tough going. Most mail-order tool companies sell simple plow planes or slightly more complicated, and more expensive, combination planes. Prices vary—from $60 to well over $100 (1985)—so shop around. The plane shown above is a Stanley #45, a more complicated molding plane that can also be used as a plow plane. I got lucky and picked it up at a garage sale for $25.

To set up the plane, make sure that the blade is razor-sharp and that the outside faces of the runners are flush with the edges of the blade. When plowing across grain, use the small spurs housed ahead of the cutter in each of the runner faces. They score the wood, which keeps the fibers from splintering on either side of the dado. The spurs should be knife-sharp and long enough to score the wood cleanly, but not so long that they tear it.

Narrow box sides are easily dadoed in pairs. Place a pair on the benchtop, inside faces up, bottom ends aligned, good edges butted together. Then clamp a wooden straightedge across them, flush with the mark for the first dado wall. Set the plane on the far edge, tight to the fence, and draw it carefully back toward you to scribe the walls with the spurs without engaging the cutter. Then chisel a ramp in the waste at the end of the dado to prevent splintering. The first few strokes establish the dado, so make them carefully—set a shallow depth of cut and keep the plane tight against the fence and perpendicular to the board's face. After two or three strokes the plane will follow its own path, so you can remove the straightedge. Most plow planes have depth stops, but I use mine only for a rough gauge; when I get down to the scribe marks on the edges, I check the depth of the groove with a steel ruler. Slide a piece of scrap into both dadoes to keep the sides aligned, and reset the fence for the next cut.

Plow-planing takes practice, so dado a

few pieces of scrap before tackling the real thing. The fussiest adjustment is aligning the edges of the cutter, the faces of the runners and the spurs to cut the dado walls cleanly. As you become familiar with the tool, you'll develop little dodges to make the job more accurate and efficient.

Tongue-and-groove corner joints are not much more difficult to cut than dadoes, just a little more time-consuming. I make the tongue about one-quarter to one-third as thick as the board, whichever matches the plow-plane cutter, router bit or dado head to be used for cutting the groove. The top and bottom of the lower box are the same length as the upper-box shelves, so the length of the tongue (the groove depth) is the same as the depth of the dadoes.

Make the groove first—it's easier to plane the tongue to fit it than vice versa. Since the tongue has a shoulder, you can make the groove just slightly deeper than the tongue length to avoid having the tongue bottom out at assembly. I plow the groove by running the plane's fence attachment against the end of the side. You could also run the plane against a clamped-on fence as you did for the dadoes. Make sure that there are no high spots on the

bottom of the groove that would keep the joint from going together completely.

The tongues, created by rabbeting the ends of the top, should fit snugly in their grooves. I cut them with a rabbet plane, a narrow plane with a blade that extends completely across the sole and with faces perpendicular to the sole. One face has a spur like that on the plow plane. (You can also rabbet with a plow plane or a shoulder plane.)

First gauge the shoulder line and tongue thickness on the ends. Use a cutting gauge (a marking gauge with a small knife instead of a pin) if you've got one, because it makes a cleaner line across grain. Position the top on the bench and clamp a wooden straightedge fence on the shoulder line to guide the plane. Alternatively, set the plane's adjustable fence to run against the end of the board. Make sure that the blade and spur are sharp, and that the blade is flush with the spur face—if it's shy of the face, the rabbet will be stepped; if it's proud of the face, the shoulder will be ragged. Draw the plane backward as before to scribe the shoulder with the spur, make a ramp at the far end of the rabbet to prevent tearout, then plane away. When I'm close to the gauge lines, I try the tongue in the groove and

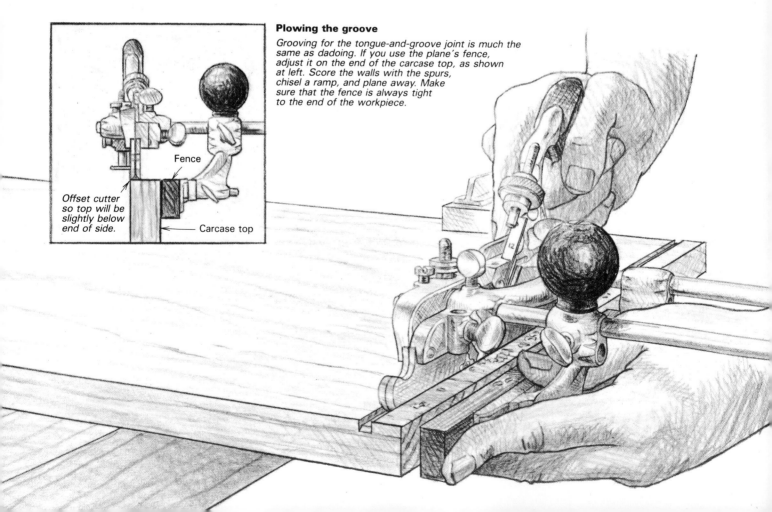

Plowing the groove

Grooving for the tongue-and-groove joint is much the same as dadoing. If you use the plane's fence, adjust it on the end of the carcase top, as shown at left. Score the walls with the spurs, chisel a ramp, and plane away. Make sure that the fence is always tight to the end of the workpiece.

Fence

Offset cutter so top will be slightly below end of side.

Carcase top

Rabbeting the tongue
As when dadoing, score the rabbet with the spur and chisel a ramp in the waste before planing. Keep the fence tight to the end, and the plane's machined spur face perpendicular to the work.

the glue, then build up from a side on the floor. Protect the surface by laying the side on a clean piece of plywood or particleboard. Spread glue in all the dadoes (and grooves) in one side with a stick or a flux brush (available at most hardware stores), making sure that the dado walls are covered. Then stick the shelves in place. Align the back edges and the rabbet before you push the ends home—it's impossible to slide an end sideways in a tight joint. Work quickly, seating each end as best you can, but don't worry if they don't go down completely; you'll pull the joint tight with clamps in a minute.

When the shelves are housed in the first side, glue the second and push it down on the shelf ends, aligning the back edges and the rabbets before driving the joints home. The second side is harder to wiggle into place—a shelf or two always wants to pop out. So I get them started, then drive them down with a hammer padded by a thick hardwood block. As you've already made sure all the joints fit, you shouldn't have any nasty surprises.

Now draw the joints tight with clamps. Getting two clamps and two cauls in place on a shelf all by yourself is exasperating—enlist a friend if you can. If you can't, figure it out dry beforehand. The top of the lower box is easier to pull tight because you can rest the clamps on it. Tight joints usually will stay in place after you've

Gluing up
Getting the shelves started in the second-side dadoes can be trying. When you've succeeded, drive them home with a hammer and wooden block.

take the final cuts to fit the joint with a sharp, finely set shoulder plane.

Cutting the rabbets for the backs is the final bit of joinery required. I cut them just slightly deeper than the ⅛-in. back and about three-quarters the thickness of the sides. I rabbeted only the sides of the boxes, and butted all the horizontal pieces against the back. Rabbet the top of the lower box if you want to hide the top edge of the back. Because the rabbet runs parallel to the grain, you needn't knife the shoulder line or use the spur cutter. If you're tapering the bookcase sides, do it now.

To make sure everything fits, put the boxes together dry before gluing up. If the shelves are all the same thickness, dry assembly should go quickly. If they're not, now is the time to fit them individually to the dadoes. I thin the ends with a sharp, finely set jointer plane, planing

with or across the grain. Be careful not to take too much off—if you're not confident with the plane, it might be better to sand off tiny amounts. You should be able to assemble the joints by hand, though it may take some wiggling to get the ends to seat all along the length of the dado. If you're fitting the joints individually, mark the end/dado pairs clearly.

When you're sure the boxes will go together, clear a space in the shop and organize the things you'll need for gluing up. You should have at least two pipe clamps and a pair of stout cauls for each box—scrap hardwood at least 1 in. by 3 in. and just a bit longer than the width of the sides will do. Plane a slight crown in the cauls for the wide sides; pressure on the ends will produce pressure in the middle. I use a white glue like Elmer's Glue-All because it sets up more slowly than yellow glue.

I lay the parts on the bench to spread

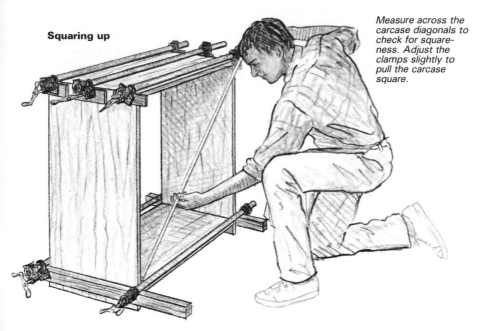

Squaring up

Measure across the carcase diagonals to check for squareness. Adjust the clamps slightly to pull the carcase square.

pulled them home; if they don't, just leave the clamps on while the glue dries.

Check the squareness of the box by measuring diagonally from corner to corner. If the diagonals aren't equal, you can adjust by pulling across the longer diagonal by hand or with a clamp (on wide boxes, clamp front and back to keep the box from twisting). Sometimes just perching the box on the floor on one corner and leaning into the diagonal corner will correct the problem—don't lean too hard, though.

When all the joints are pulled tight, carefully set the box on its side on the floor for nailing. Nails help keep the joints tight while the glue sets, and they add a certain amount of strength, particularly if the joints are at all loose. (If the joints are less than a friction fit, I'd reinforce them with screws.) Check for squareness, then drive in some finishing nails at a slight angle. Flip the box over and nail the other side.

If you're adding a back, do it now before the glue sets. A square, well-fitted back will help square up most boxes. Flush any uneven joints between shelf edges and rabbets with a chisel or plane. I painted the inside face of the back before assembly. To assemble, run a bead of glue down the rabbets and across the edges of the shelves—not too much or it will squeeze out—and nail the back in place. If the box is out of square, nail along one side first, then force the other side square as you nail it down. For extra strength, I nailed a 1-in. by 2½-in. kickboard to the sides and bottom as shown on p. 14.

Let any squeezed-out glue set to a rubbery consistency, then pare it off with a

sharp chisel. If you don't want to hang around waiting, swab off squeeze-out with a damp rag, but remember that finish won't take on those areas without thorough sanding. When the glue is dry, flush off the joints with a sharp plane. I chamfered the edges and corners of the boxes with a piloted chamfer bit and router; files and a block plane will do the job as well, if more slowly. The floors in our house are like roller coasters, so I routed out a segment of the bottom ends of the lower-box sides to make four small feet. A coping saw and spokeshave would work, too.

Adjustable shelves perch quite adequately on ¼-in. dowel shelf pegs. I made a Masonite template for the holes in the lower box; resting it on the bottom and flush with the back ensured that the holes would be in the same locations on each side. A piece of tape wrapped around the twist drill or auger bit serves as a dandy depth gauge to keep you from inadvertently drilling through the sides. I chamfered the holes with a countersink bit because I think it looks nice and it makes inserting the dowels easier.

Like all simple, quick projects, this one took me about twice as long as I had expected, so I was in no mood to apply a complicated finish. Which was just as well, because I think film finishes (varnishes and lacquers) generally make pine look terrible. A couple of coats of Johnson's Paste Wax seem to protect the surfaces well enough, and I could enlist the whole family's help in putting it on. □

Roger Holmes is an associate editor at Fine Woodworking.

Machines do it, too

Dadoes: To dado the sides on a tablesaw, set up the dado head to match the thickness of the shelves (or you can thickness the shelves to match the dado). Dado a piece of scrap and try the shelves. I fine-tune the dado width by adding donut-shaped paper shims of various thicknesses between the cutters. Set the depth for about one-third the thickness of the side.

I run the ends of the sides against the rip fence to cut the dadoes—one setting cuts the two dadoes for each shelf. I find this a faster method than using a miter gauge, and it ensures that the shelves are square to the ends. Use a miter gauge for dadoing boards less than 6 in. wide, and for dadoes in the middle of sides too long to be passed against the fence.

With the dado head set up and the fence positioned for the bottom shelf, dado both carcase sides. Most saw guards have to be removed for dadoing, so work carefully, keeping your hands well clear of the blade. Narrow boards can be tricky because there isn't much surface bearing against the fence. I find that placing my right hand near the fence as shown in the drawing below helps overcome any tendency of the board to pivot during the cut. If you're at all uneasy with this procedure, use a miter gauge to steady the board. Push the board's inside face down

Tablesawn dadoes

One fence setting cuts matching dadoes in a pair of identical, squared-up sides.

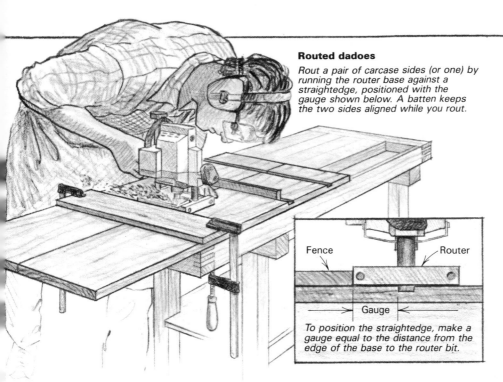

Routed dadoes

Rout a pair of carcase sides (or one) by running the router base against a straightedge, positioned with the gauge shown below. A batten keeps the two sides aligned while you rout.

Fence   Router

Gauge

To position the straightedge, make a gauge equal to the distance from the edge of the base to the router bit.

Tongues: You can rout the rabbet that creates the tongue by running the router base against a straightedge as for routing a dado. Rabbet a piece of scrap exactly the same thickness as the top to check bit depth. The tongue should be a snug fit in the groove, as for dadoes.

The drawback of this method is that if the top isn't uniformly thick, the tongue won't be either. The tablesaw method shown below overcomes this problem. Set up the saw with a single sharp cross-cut or combination blade. Cut the shoulder first, running the end against the fence, the outside face down on the table. Make the same cut in several pieces of scrap to use for setting up the second cut.

For this second setup, the distance between the fence and the blade should equal the tongue's thickness, which eliminates the need for uniform thickness. Adding a tall wooden fence to the rip fence will help you keep the top perpendicular to the table. Few boards are dead flat, so I clamp a wide feather board to the saw table, positioned so the pressure it exerts will push the top flush to the fence for several inches on both sides of the blade. Test the setup on the scrap, then cut the real thing. (Stand to one side as you complete the cuts, in case the saw kicks the waste back.)   —*R.H.*

on the table so the dadoes will be uniformly deep. (Waxing the table and fence also helps.) After cutting the first pair of dadoes, reset the fence and cut the next pair and so on. (If you're making adjustable shelves, dado for the top shelf now and you're done.)

I work off one end to about the middle, then work from the other end. If the sides are square, this shouldn't cause any problems. Most tablesaws can clear up to 24 in. between the blade and fence, so this procedure will work for bookshelves up to 4 ft. tall.

Dadoes can be routed by guiding the router base against a straightedge. First make a gauge for positioning the fence, as shown in the drawing above. Narrow sides can be routed in pairs. Lay them inside-faces-up on a flat surface, aligned and tight together. Clamp the straightedge below and parallel to the first dado, positioning it with your scrapwood gauge. Rout the first dado, slide a scrapwood batten into the grooves to keep the sides aligned, and repeat the procedure for the next dado. If your router base is round, always run the same spot against the fence unless you're sure the base is concentric with the bit.

With a little thought, you can figure out various easily made jigs to speed up the process. Without them, however, I think the tablesaw is faster—it's a ready-made jig for positioning the cuts.

Grooves: On the tablesaw, set up the dado head to the right thickness and height, and run the end of the side against the fence as for dadoing. Position the groove slightly farther from

the end than the thickness of the top so you have only to plane off a little end grain to clean up the joint after assembly. If you rout the groove, guide the router base against a clamped-on fence as for dadoing, or use the adjustable fence that comes as an accessory on most routers.

Tablesawn tongues

Lay the workpiece flat on the table for the first cut. Run it end-up against the fence as shown here for the second.

Fence   Workpiece

Feather board

Blade

First cut

Starting Out
Build and fit a basic drawer

by Roger Holmes

I have always been fond of cabinets filled with row upon row of little drawers, each cleanly dovetailed and snugly fitted in its opening. Drawers seem full of promise and mystery. When they're closed, that is; an open drawer usually reveals much more junk than treasure. But there is pleasure in sliding open a well-made and well-fitted drawer, even if it's filled with shoelaces and paper clips.

Making drawers can be fun, too, if you don't let your ambition outstrip your ability. I'll never forget the sight of my first attempt, a little drawer barely three inches deep, buried beneath a network of pipe clamps attached in a vain attempt to pull its ill-fitting dovetails tight and its corners square. The drawer joinery shown here is more modest, but perfectly adequate. Using it will allow you to get the hang of making a drawer square and fitting it to a cabinet before you stir dovetails into the mix. And if you need lots of drawers, these are quick to make. Drawers are also well suited for mass production—if you're making more than one, do the same operation on all the pieces at the same time.

The fit of a drawer in a cabinet can be as important as the construction of the drawer itself. I always make the carcase first and then the drawers to fit it. The ideal is a snug fit, with drawer sides and carcase sides sliding against each other like the walls of a piston and its cylinder (well, as much like a piston and cylinder as your patience and the material allow). But the drawer will work even if it is looser, so fitting a drawer really well is a challenge more than a necessity—a distinction worth remembering after you've fiddled around for an unsuccessful hour trying to do it. I use the method described below when I'm trying for that ideal fit; for a less refined and much quicker method, see the box on p. 24.

The drawer joinery—locking tongue-and-groove at the front corners, dadoes for the back and sides—is a variation on the carcase joinery described in "Starting Out: Simple bookcase joints" (see pp. 14-19). I've hung the drawer on runners housed in its sides, which is less traditional than resting the drawer on a frame (a rail under the drawer front, runners under the

sides). Frames can stiffen a carcase, and I use at least one or two in tall stacks of wide drawers. Side-hanging the drawers saves time (no frames to make) as well as the space taken up by the frames, which can be as much as 3 in. on a four-drawer cabinet. The method below, however, can be used to fit either type of drawer.

I made the drawers of pine, but it's not the best-wearing wood for drawer sides—a hard wood would be better. Boards with growth rings more or less parallel to the edges when viewed on the end grain (called quartersawn or riftsawn) are least likely to cup and shrink, and are worth culling out of your lumber pile for use as drawer sides.

Accurate stock preparation is the key to successful drawermaking. If the parts aren't square, the drawer won't be either. Cut all the fronts, backs and sides roughly to size: front and back about $\frac{1}{32}$ in. longer than the distance between the carcase sides; drawer sides about 1 in. less than the width of the carcase sides. I make the fronts $\frac{3}{4}$ in. thick; the backs and sides

A side-hung drawer

This drawer is easy to make and hang in a new or existing carcase.
It's fitted so its sides slide smoothly against the carcase sides.

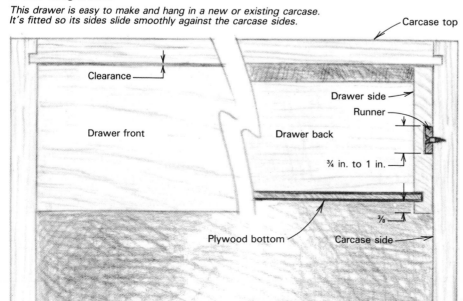

Clearance

Drawer front

Carcase top

Drawer side

Runner

Drawer back

¾ in. to 1 in.

Plywood bottom

⅜

Carcase side

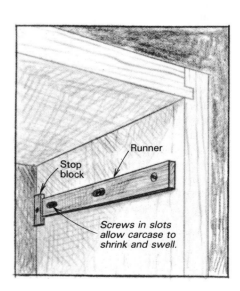

Stop block

Runner

Screws in slots allow carcase to shrink and swell.

From *Fine Woodworking* magazine (March 1985) 51: 58-62

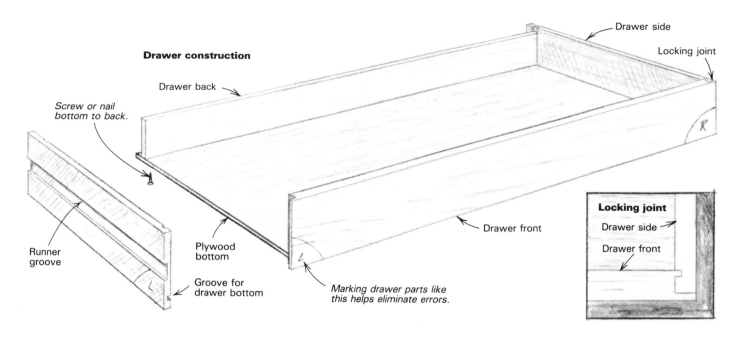

Drawer construction

Drawer side

Locking joint

Drawer back

Screw or nail bottom to back.

Runner groove

Plywood bottom

Groove for drawer bottom

Drawer front

Marking drawer parts like this helps eliminate errors.

Locking joint

Drawer side

Drawer front

about ½ in. thick. Take care when flattening the pieces—twisted parts make twisted drawers. The back is dadoed to the sides, so match its thickness to a standard plowplane blade or router bit.

Mark the good faces, then plane and mark the good edges on all the boards, checking them with a straightedge. I put the good edges on the bottom of the drawer. (A simple way to keep the pieces straight is shown above.) The ends of the pieces *must* be square to the good edges. If they're not, the drawer will certainly be twisted, and probably not be square. I usually do this planing freehand, holding the piece end-up in the vise and checking squareness with a try square or a framing square.

A shooting board, shown in the drawing at right, is a good jig for doing the same thing, particularly if you're making lots of drawers. There's not much to a shooting board, but it must be made accurately; obviously the stop must be dead square to the guiding edge, and the sole of your plane perpendicular to the plane's sides. Use whatever plane is most comfortable for you. I use my jointer plane because of its weight and long bearing surface. (No, you won't plane the guiding edge as well as the workpiece.) Fool around squaring up scrapwood until you get the hang of the shooting board.

Square the ends of the drawer front first, planing enough off so that the front will just about, but not quite, fit between the carcase sides. Only the front end of each drawer side need be square for this construction; if you're corner-jointing the back to the sides as well, square up both ends. Unless you're sure of the dado

depths now, plane the back to exact length after you dado the sides.

Next groove the inside faces of the sides and front for the drawer bottom (it passes under the back). You can plow the grooves with a plow plane, rout them, or cut them on the tablesaw with a dado head. They shouldn't be deeper than half the thickness of the pieces. I locate them ⅜ in. above the

bottom edges, which leaves enough wood for strength without stealing too much depth from the drawer. Remember to run the bottom, good edge against the fence of whatever tool you use for grooving.

The locking joints at the front corners are a little more complicated than those for the carcase. (If you used the simple car-

Shooting board

You can square an end to an edge quickly and accurately with a shooting board, one of the simplest of jigs.

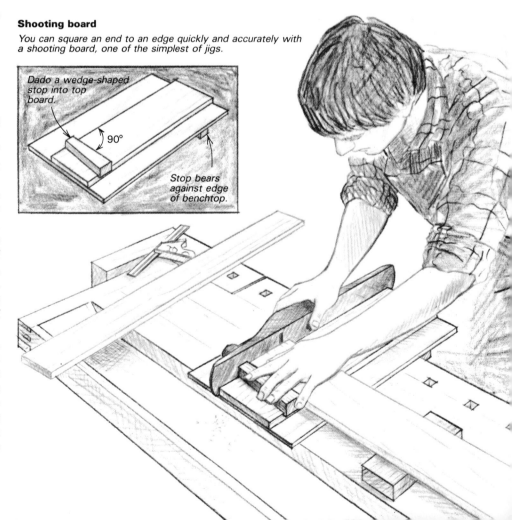

Dado a wedge-shaped stop into top board.

90°

Stop bears against edge of benchtop.

case joint shown on p. 20 for the drawers, either the end grain of the sides would show, or the tongue would have to be on the sides, running in the direction of most stress—the front would easily pull away from the sides.) This joint is fairly easy to cut on the tablesaw or with a plow plane, but I think it's too much trouble to rout. Regardless of how you cut the joint, do it accurately, because its strength depends on a close mating of the parts.

The drawings at right show proportions and the sequence of cuts on the tablesaw. I use a single blade that cuts a kerf about $\frac{5}{32}$ in. wide, which is sufficient width for the groove. Make the groove depth (cut **1**) about one-third the thickness of the side. Make cut **2** using the same fence setting as for cut **1** to ensure that the end of the drawer side will fit tight against the drawer-front rabbet. Cut the front and several pieces of scrap the same thickness as the front, then use the scrap to reset the fence for cut **3** to make a snug-fitting tongue. I make the final cut just shy of the groove bottom, so the tongue won't bottom out and hold the joint apart.

Though this is essentially a machine joint, it can be cut by hand with a plow plane as shown. I use a $\frac{1}{4}$-in. cutter to groove the side (**B**) and a $\frac{5}{16}$-in. cutter for the end of the front (**A**). Plow the groove in the side first, setting the fence using the wider cutter as a gauge. Plug the drawer-bottom groove with a tight-fitting scrap to prevent breaking it out, and remember to chisel ramps at the ends of the cuts to prevent tearout. To make the tongue, set the plow-plane fence using the groove cutter as a gauge. Plowing in end grain, at least in soft woods, isn't much more difficult than plowing with the grain, but practice on some scrap first.

Dado the sides for the drawer back with tablesaw and dado head, router, or plow plane. I place the dado about $\frac{1}{2}$ in. to 1 in. from the end of the side, so there's plenty of wood on both sides of the dado for strength. One-third the thickness of the side is sufficient depth.

Next groove the outside faces of the drawer sides for the runners. The width of the runners isn't critical; I find that $\frac{3}{4}$-in. to 1-in. wide runners are easier to work with than narrower runners, and probably stiffer. I make the runner grooves $\frac{3}{16}$ in. to $\frac{1}{4}$ in. deep, and plow them from end to end—the drawer front will cover the groove at the front end. For drawers up to 6 in. deep, center the grooves; for deeper drawers, locate them nearer the top edge.

I think that solid-wood bottoms give a

Tablesawn locking joint
The locking joint can be cut quickly and accurately by following this sequence of cuts.

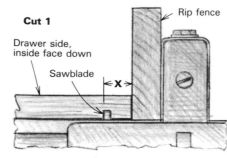

Cut 1

Rip fence
Drawer side, inside face down
Sawblade
X

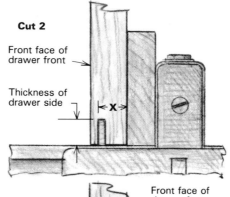

Cut 2
Front face of drawer front
Thickness of drawer side
X

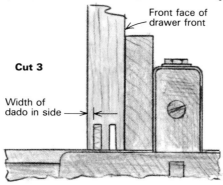

Cut 3
Front face of drawer front
Width of dado in side

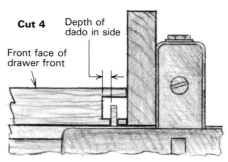

Cut 4
Depth of dado in side
Front face of drawer front

*Lay out a tablesawn joint according to the sawblade thickness, as shown at left below. Lay out a plow-plane joint to match standard cutters (**A** and **B**).*

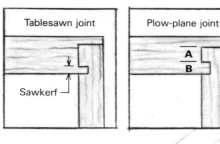

Tablesawn joint
Sawkerf

Plow-plane joint
A
B

drawer a nice heft, and raise it a notch or two in quality, but they're sure a lot more work than plywood bottoms. When I make solid bottoms, I plane them about $\frac{5}{16}$ in. or $\frac{3}{8}$ in. thick, then thin them at the edges with a bevel or a rabbet to fit the grooves. Whether the bottom is solid wood or plywood, trim it square and fit it snugly from side to side, and so it runs beneath the drawer back. The grain of a solid-wood bottom should parallel the drawer front so it won't shrink out of the side grooves, or push the sides apart when it expands. Grain direction doesn't matter for plywood bottoms, but I run it parallel to the front anyway.

All the parts should be ready for assembly now, but first I clean up the inside faces of everything and wax them, taking care not to get wax on a surface to be glued. It's a lot easier to do this now than later. If you want more protection than wax but not a full-blown finish, brush on a coat of sanding sealer, rub it down with steel wool, then wax it.

Assembly is straightforward, but it's not a bad idea to make a dry run just to see that everything fits, and that you've got all the clamps and paraphernalia you'll need. Then spread glue in the groove and dado of one side, and insert the front and back, aligning the grooves for the bottom. Slide in the bottom and add the second side. (You can glue plywood in place, but a

Hand-planed locking joint
You can cut a locking joint with a plow plane. The drawer front is being plowed here.

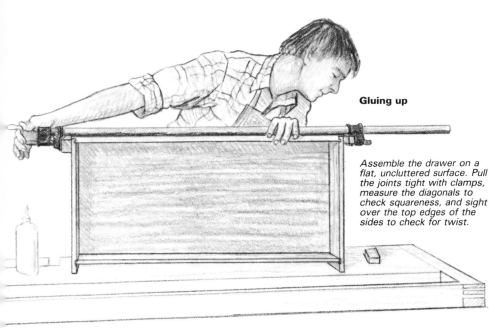

Gluing up

Assemble the drawer on a flat, uncluttered surface. Pull the joints tight with clamps, measure the diagonals to check squareness, and sight over the top edges of the sides to check for twist.

solid bottom should just be nailed or screwed to the back.) Assembling with the drawer bottom in place helps keep the drawer square. Pull the joints tight with pipe clamps, placing hardwood blocks between the jaws and the sides to protect the surfaces and distribute the clamping pressure. You can leave the clamps on while the glue sets, or drive a couple of nails in each joint and take them off.

Measure the diagonals to check for squareness. Sight over the edges of the sides or try to rock the drawer on the benchtop to see if it is twisted. If it is, you can weight the high corners; too much counter-twisting can break the joints. If the twist isn't too bad, you can plane it out when fitting the drawer to the carcase. If you find yourself planing off most of the drawer side, make another drawer. Leave the drawer on a flat surface while the glue dries.

The runners for the drawers are best made of a hard wood such as maple, cherry or oak. The easiest way to make them is to thickness a wide board to a sliding fit in the runner grooves and rip the runners off the edge. Plane the edge of the wide board after each cut so each runner will have one smooth face. I make the runners just slightly thinner than the depth of the runner grooves and about ¾ in. shorter than the drawer sides.

The runners are slot-screwed to the carcase sides to allow the sides to shrink and expand with changes in humidity. In better-quality work, the runners are housed in dadoes in the carcase sides, then screwed down. I think three #6 screws are sufficient to fasten a 15-in. runner. The screw

near the front end is fixed through a single hole so it won't move in relation to the front edge of the carcase. I make each slot by boring two holes ½ in. apart and chiseling out the waste in between. (Save a little time by boring the holes in the edge of the wide board before ripping off the individual runners.) Countersink the holes and slots so the screwheads will be beneath the runner's surface.

To install the runners, make a gauge block equal in width to the distance from the top of the runner groove to the top edge of the drawer side, as shown in the drawing below. This distance should be the same for each pair of sides on a draw-

Attaching the runners

Make a runner gauge as shown below, then butt the gauge against the carcase top to position the runner while you screw it in place.

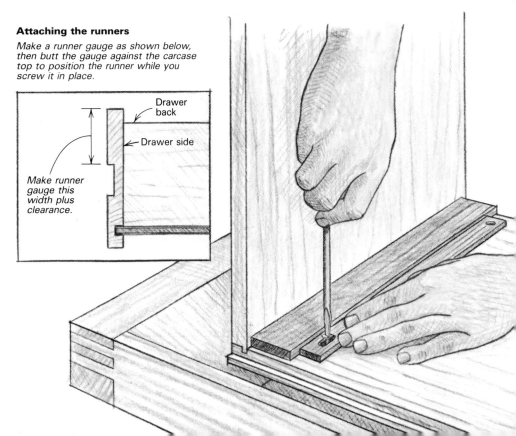

Drawer back

Drawer side

Make runner gauge this width plus clearance.

er. The block should be about as long as the carcase is deep. Lay the carcase on its side, butt the gauge into the upper corner, position the runner against the gauge about ½ in. back from the carcase's front edge, and screw the runner in place. (You'll need to bore pilot holes for the screws in hardwood carcase sides.)

The drawer sides and front will expand and contract across their width with changes in humidity. You can allow for this in the gauge, or by adding a spacer between the gauge and the carcase top, or by planing the sides down when fitting. The size of the gap will vary according to the wood used and the conditions where you live. In England, we used to fit drawers in fine work very closely because the humidity was fairly constant year round. On my first job after returning to Nebraska, I fitted the drawers tightly, only to have to plane the height of the sides later to accommodate the extreme variation in humidity from summer to winter—4-in. deep riftsawn oak sides moved more than ⅛ in. across their width. Play it safe on your first drawers.

Now you're ready to fit the drawer to the carcase. With luck, this will require only a couple of fine shavings off each drawer side and just a touch from a sanding block on the bottom edge of the runners. An assembled drawer is difficult to hold in a vise, so I clamp a piece of ¾-in. plywood to the benchtop to support the drawer for planing. The width of the ply should fit easily inside the drawer, and the

A simple slider

If you're not too bothered by how a drawer looks, or not quite so compulsive about how it fits, try this method. The sides, front and back are joined exactly the same as for the drawer on p. 20, but you don't need to groove for the bottom and the runners. Make the drawer bottom of ¼-in. or ⅜-in. plywood—Baltic birch if you can afford it, or an interior grade that permits few voids if you can't; ¼-in. tempered Masonite will work, too. The width of the drawer isn't terribly important. I leave a ⅛-in. gap between the carcase sides and the drawer sides. (A large gap like this, uniform on both sides, announces itself as deliberate, and shouldn't raise any eyebrows.) I assemble the sides, back and front, then glue and nail the bottom in place after making sure it slides easily in the carcase dadoes.

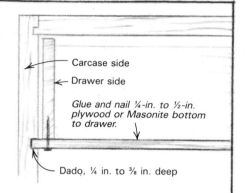

Carcase side

Drawer side

Glue and nail ¼-in. to ½-in. plywood or Masonite bottom to drawer.

Dado, ¼ in. to ⅜ in. deep

You can dado the carcase sides to accept the drawer bottom before assembling the carcase or after. If you do it after, dado before attaching the back. Either way, you'll need to fix a fence to the carcase side to guide the router or plow plane. A good trick is to make the top drawer as deep as the distance from the edge of the router base to the bit—just run the base against the carcase top to cut the dadoes.   —R.H.

Planing the sides

Clamp a piece of plywood to the bench so it overhangs the edge enough to support the drawer for planing. Plane and sand down the sides carefully, from back to front, until the drawer slips easily but snugly into the carcase.

piece should overhang the edge of the bench by about the drawer's depth.

The initial goal when fitting is to get the drawer to slide completely into the carcase, as tight to the sides as possible. Using a sharp plane, first take a thin shaving off the back half of both drawer sides, then try the drawer in the opening. If it fits halfway, plane farther forward until it fits all the way; if it doesn't fit halfway, take more off the back. If the drawer gets hung up, remember to check the runners, too. More than once, I've planed too much off a drawer side before discovering a sticky spot on a runner. You can trim the runners with a sharp, finely set shoulder plane, or with sandpaper wrapped tightly around a square-edged block of hardwood.

When the drawer slides completely into the carcase, work the sides and runners with planes or sandpaper until it slides sweetly. Colored chalk rubbed on the carcase sides will show up high spots on the drawer sides. Finally, paste-wax all the mating surfaces. You should be able to open and shut a well-fitted drawer with only your little finger, and when the drawer is halfway out, there should be very little movement either up and down or side to side.

When the drawer fits, screw stop blocks at the back of the carcase to fix its position when closed. If the drawer front is allowed to strike the end of the runners to stop the drawer, the front will soon be popped off. (The runners are acceptable drawer stops if you stop the runner grooves about 1 in. short of the drawer front.) I like the drawer front to sit about ⅛ in. back from the edge of the carcase. To add another drawer, or a stack of drawers, just repeat the process, gauging from the drawer above to place the runners.

This all sounds like a lot of trouble, you might say, for a simple pine drawer. True, there's no need to fit this drawer with anything like the precision I've described. For that matter, there's no need to fit any drawer like this. I have drawers in my house that you can practically throw into their openings from across the room, and they still do a fine job of corralling my socks and shirts. But if your dream is to someday build one of those exquisite cabinets with lots of piston-fit little drawers, then the more practice you have, even with humble pine drawers, the more likely you are to succeed when it really matters to you.   □

Roger Holmes is an associate editor at Fine Woodworking.

Dragonfly

Plans for a cam-operated pull toy

by William Huntley

The cam is a marvel of mechanical simplicity, transforming circular motion into linear, and vice versa, with basically two moving parts. It transmits the driving force to mechanical devices from bicycles to locomotives. When used in a finely finished wooden toy it can provide motion to stimulate and enchant the imagination.

I stumbled onto the cam wheel several years ago when designing my first pull toy, a wooden rabbit that hopped on two eccentrically mounted wheels. From hopping rabbits and frogs through wiggling fish, I came to the push rod—to flap wings and agitate jointed legs. The inspiration for designing a toy dragonfly came from the river behind my workshop. Darting and hovering, with bodies straight and rigid, their rapidly beating wings create that same slow-motion effect seen in a whirlybird propeller. The dragonfly seemed perfect for mechanical rendering, and the model in the plans on the next page has been in production more than a year.

The first problem was how to add an assortment of mechanical apparatus to a six-legged, four-winged creature. To avoid visual clutter, I gave the animal only four legs, using them to support two sets of axles and wheels. The wings are hinged inside the block of wood that is the abdomen, with smooth curves taking the sharpness from external mechanical parts. After several experiments with wheel diameter and push-rod length, a working model emerged. In production I make dragonflies in batches of 10, but I'll describe the procedure as if I were making only one.

The three main sections of the dragonfly are made separately and doweled together, carefully matching the shapes of abutting pieces at each joint. I cut the blanks for the head, abdomen and thorax from the same piece of 2-in. by 3⅛-in. walnut or mahogany. This allows a continuous matching of grain and color through the body. I drill the dowel holes centered in the ends of the rectangular blanks, then rough-shape each part by bandsawing in two steps. I start with the side-view profile and save the cutaway pieces for support in making the second cut to obtain the outline of the overview. It's important that the layout of all shapes be centered on the dowel holes, because inaccuracies are exaggerated by the long, slender body.

The angled sides of the head, to which the eyes are glued, are a little tricky to cut. First, I lay out the tapered shape on the bottom side of the head with two straight lines from points 2 in. apart at the rear edge of the stock to a thickness of ¾ in. at the tip. I cut along these straight lines, cradling the head in the top cutaway produced in the profile cut.

The layout and machining of the abdomen are the most critical part of the procedure. This piece contains all the moving parts, which must be accurately aligned to ensure smooth operation. All machining for the legs and wing assembly is done before shaping this piece. First, I rip a ½-in. thickness off the top side of the dimensioned blank. This piece will be

replaced over the wing hinges and secured during bandsawing and shaping with blind dowels. Next I bandsaw the rectangular cutouts and mill the slots that will receive the dowels on which the wings pivot. For the milling I use a tool slide salvaged from a metal lathe. It consists of a small sliding table with two stop adjustments similar to the one on a drill press. The slide is controlled by a geared lever and contains several *T*-slots to which a vise may be bolted. The slide and vise assembly is then clamped to a drill-press table. With a straight, ¼-in. router bit chucked in the spindle, and with the spindle turning at its highest speed, this setup can produce straight and accurate slots. The spindle is lowered to a fixed height, and the lever moves the work horizontally into the bit. This rig is useful for accurate mortising and for drilling a series of holes along a centerline, especially in round stock.

I shape the roughed-out parts with a stationary belt sander, rasps and a flap sander. The belt sander takes out band-saw marks and roughs out the curves and contours on the sharp edges. Several rasps and a flap sander with 100-grit abrasive produce the finished shape. A table-mounted router with a self-piloting, quarter-round bit gives the thorax a ½-in. radius. Positioning the piece with the convex side toward the table, I make several shallow cuts until I reach the desired radius. The outside edges of the wheels are similarly shaped with the router, using a ⅜-in. radius cutter.

I have found that a circle-cutting jig and band saw make good wheels and other round parts. My jig uses a sharp, hard-steel point as a pivot pin. Rounds are cut quickly and accurately and emerge with the center marked. I edge-sand wheels on the lathe, using a tapered arbor held in a chuck. With a

Huntley's menagerie: Turtle of laminated maple shell and mahogany head/tail and legs is the only one not cam-operated. It is a bank, and a coin dropped through the slot in its shell causes the head and tail to bob. The rabbit hops; the stack-laminated, mahogany beaver with the ivory teeth flaps its tail; the butterfly of six different woods flutters its wings; the fish wiggles its jointed tail and waves its fins.

From *Fine Woodworking* magazine (November 1979) 19:61-63

Two Toy Trucks

Auto transport and delivery vans

by William J. Lavin

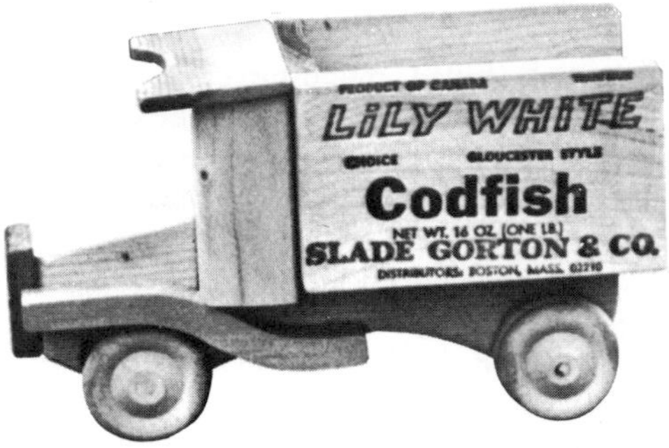
LILY WHITE
Codfish
SLADE GORTON & CO.

The auto transport is a favorite of both the youngster who plays with it and the grandparent or parent who builds it. The unit functions as a toy truck, and the vehicles it carries are toys, too. The truck rolls and turns, and the top carrier slants down to unload. Inlet grooves cut into the ramps allow the vehicles to remain in place over the bumpiest of roads and while the top ramp is in the unloading position.

Construction is divided into three parts: the cab, the carrier and the five vehicles. Of these, the carrier requires the most careful planning and layout.

Begin by gluing up enough stock to a thickness of 3½ in. Shape the cab and bore a hole for a window. Next make the carrier. It is divided into three units: the top and bottom ramps, the pivotal supports and the wheel/axle assembly. To make the wheel/axle assembly, prepare a piece of ¾-in. stock the combined length of the front and rear axle holders (16 in.) and lay out where the dadoes for the axles should go. Dadoes along the full width of the truck minimize axle breakage, while allowing free movement. Cut the dadoes about 1/16 in. wider and deeper than the diameter of the axles. I use ⅜-in. dowel and cut my dadoes 7/16 in. wide by 7/16 in. deep. Make sure to lay out the dadoes for double wheels far enough apart so the wheels won't rub against each other. To separate this assembly from the lower ramp, glue it to a spacer made out of 5/4 stock.

The four pivotal supports of the carrier are all the same shape but the front pair (which is stationary) is drilled differently from the rear pair (which moves). The rear support braces the top ramp and also swings down to allow the top ramp to tilt and touch the bottom ramp for car removal. The front support allows the top ramp to pivot. Carefully plan the location and size of the support holes. I secure the front pair of supports to the lower ramp with dowels, either blind or showing for decoration.

I use ¾-in. stock 2¾ in. wide for the top and bottom ramps, and cut wheel grooves into them. The wheels of the cars determine the size of the grooves. My cars have 1½-in. diameter wheels and I cut the radius of the grooves ¾ in. The diagram below shows how. I usually make two trucks at a time and clamp two pieces of stock for the top ramps (cut to size and marked with the centerlines) with ¾-in. thick scrap in between. I then bore holes with a 1½-in. speed-bore bit to a depth that will allow the wheels to rest in the groove, usually about ⅝ in. on each edge. Repeat the procedure for the bottom ramp. If you're making only one truck, use a piece of scrap that is 1½ in. thick. After the grooves are drilled, cut the

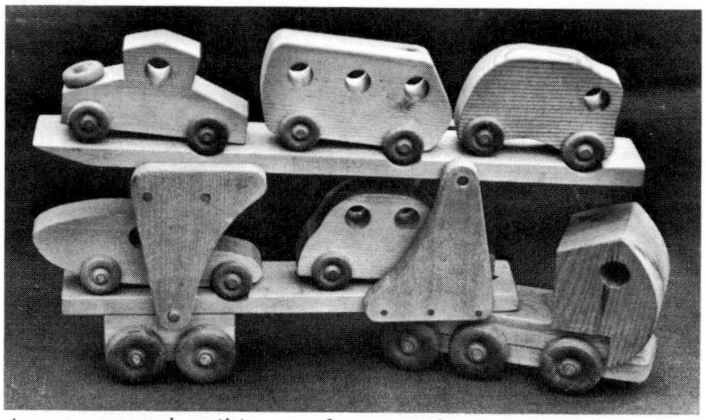

Auto transport has tilting top for easy unloading.

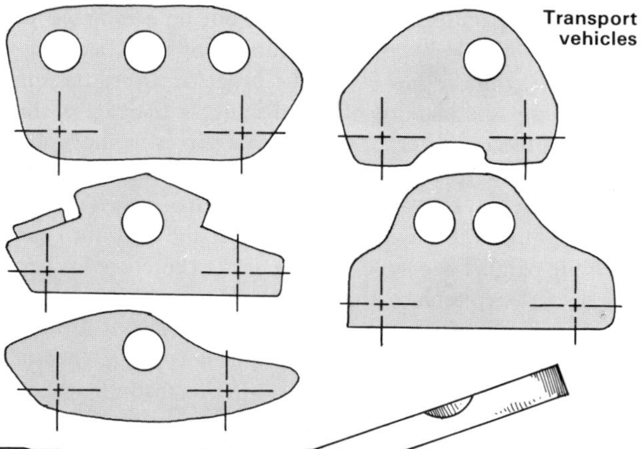
Transport vehicles

Wheel grooves cut on ramp hold cars

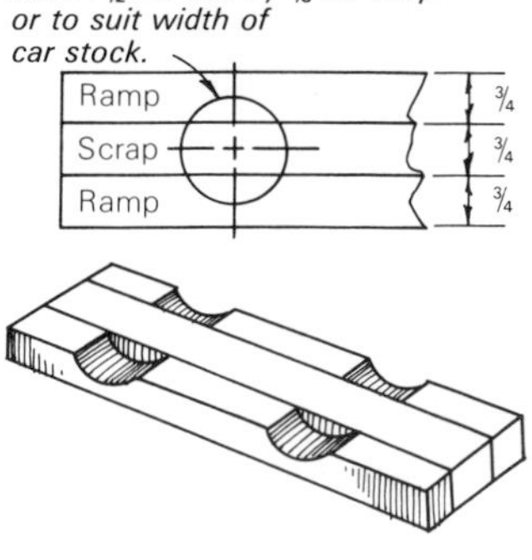
Bore 1½ in. dia. by ⅝ in. deep or to suit width of car stock.
Ramp
Scrap
Ramp
¾
¾
¾

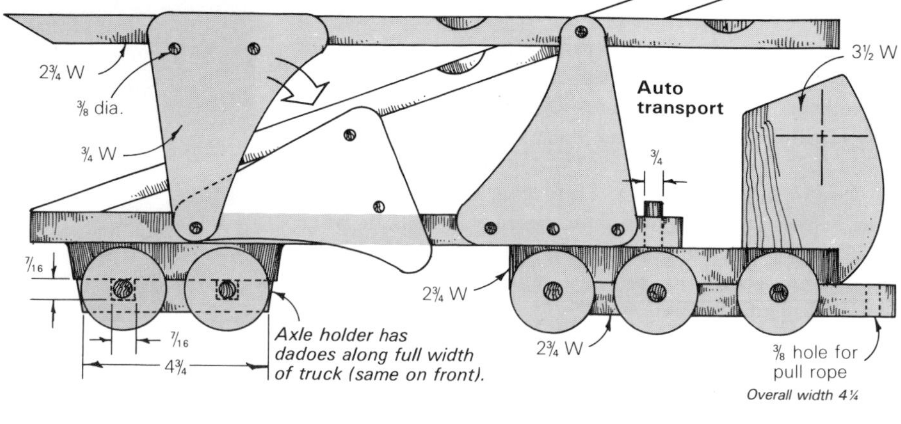
Auto transport
2¾ W
⅜ dia.
¾ W
3½ W
¾
7/16
7/16
4¾
Axle holder has dadoes along full width of truck (same on front).
2¾ W
2¾ W
⅜ hole for pull rope
Overall width 4¼

Photos: William Lavin; Illustrations: Bob Crosby

taper on the bottom side of the rear of the top ramp so that it will sit flat on the bottom ramp when slanted.

The five vehicles are cut from 1½-in. stock. Because these toys are handled so much, round all sharp edges and sand smooth the insides of all large holes. I use ¼-in. diameter axles and bore the holes ⁹⁄₃₂ in. for free movement.

Now the wheels, which is the most troublesome aspect of making toy trucks. Of all the methods I've tried, I find the best way to make the wheels is with a circle cutter on the drill press. After you cut them out, put a threaded rod the same diameter as the pilot drill on the circle cutter (usually ¼ in.) through the wheel, locking the wheel in place with a nut on either side. Chuck the assembly in the drill press and sand the rotating wheel until it's perfectly smooth. Then redrill to the axle size. Or, you can buy wheels ready-made. I get mine from Love-Built (P.O. Box 5459, Tahoe City, Calif. 95730) and use #7 wheels on the truck and #8 wheels on the vehicles. About the only time I make my own wheels is when I want them to be made out of a wood that contrasts with the body of the vehicle.

I glue the wheels onto the axles with Elmer's yellow glue. I have no problem with them falling off—in fact, in trying to remove a wheel, I've inadvertently broken the axle because the wheel wouldn't budge.

Instead of the dadoed wheel/axle assembly, you could use capped axle pegs to mount the wheels to the vehicles (also available from Love-Built, #PPLR:2). This method is not as strong, but it is much faster and easier. Simply drill a hole in the body the size of the mushroom-shaped axle peg (you want a tight press-fit), slip the peg through a wheel, and glue the peg in.

Axle pegs are also available for use on the front and rear pivotal supports (#PPLR:4). Remember that the hole at the vertex of the supports should allow free movement of the supports on the axle peg so the ramp can slant.

*   *   *

Small delivery trucks are the envy of any little boy or girl. Alphabet blocks, logs, empty boxes and almost any other imaginative cargo travel along the playland highways in these vans. It's easy to produce a fleet of them by making basic solid chassis and fitting them with shapes and styles of truck bodies not from the children's make-believe world, but from the real, everyday world of commerce. I try to use imaginative preprinted wood components—some of my truck bodies are built from the tops of 1-lb. salted codfish boxes, wooden paint-mixing sticks, wooden rules, pencils glued three or four high to form a rail, and the "does it really work?" mousetrap for the novelty approach.

To construct the chassis, I lay out several pieces of stock 1½ in. to 2 in. thick and bandsaw them to shape. I lay out the fenders on contrasting ¾-in. stock and cut them on the bandsaw, too. Then I cut the cab roof and the radiator. I always try to dress up the radiator by cutting a design into it. The cab is cut from the same stock as the chassis and has the top end slanted a few degrees forward to allow the roof to tilt down. Shallow holes can be bored in the cab for windows or you can put in plugs cut with a plug cutter from a contrasting wood. A wooden button can be used as a radiator cap on the engine. All sharp edges should be thoroughly sanded or routed with a rounding-over bit.

I use 2-in. diameter Love-Built wheels (#WP-11). These have a ¼-in. axle hole, so drill a ⁹⁄₃₂-in. hole in the chassis. I

Truck chassis stays the same; body variations include doweled flat-bed, above, and delivery van on previous page.

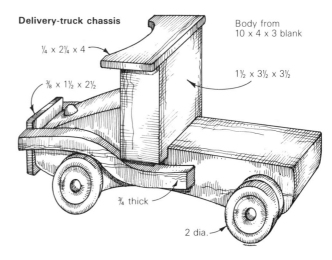

Delivery-truck chassis

¼ × 2¼ × 4

⅜ × 1½ × 2½

Body from 10 × 4 × 3 blank

1½ × 3½ × 3½

¾ thick

2 dia.

always put dual wheels on the rear for that "official-look-of-a-truck" effect.

Unless I build a body for a specific item (such as alphabet blocks), I eyeball all measurements, mark a line and cut, using one piece as a comparison for the next. What is pleasing to the eye and fits the prepainted stock is good enough. If the stock is thin, brace it by gluing it to ¼-in. or ⅜-in. backing. I glue most of the bodies to the chassis, but for the mousetrap, I rout a rabbet in the side of the truck and let the trap in. Usually the bodies are about 6 in. to 7 in. long, 4 in. to 5 in. wide, and 2 in. to 5 in. high. Be sure to release the springs on the mousetraps and fasten all metal parts securely by soldering or epoxy.

Finishing—When I know a toy will be used with all the gusto children have, I finish it with a half-and-half mixture of boiled linseed oil and pure turpentine. I brush the mixture on and after a few hours wipe it dry. I dip the wheels into the mixture. Four days later, I repeat. I have found this the best method of finishing toys: There is no grain raising between coats, and the oil brings out the grain of the wood. I often spray the delivery trucks with several light coats of Deft instead of coating them with the mixture, but don't brush the Deft on printed wood or the ink will run. □

William Lavin builds wooden toys and hand planes, and teaches junior high school industrial arts in Camillus, N.Y.

English Oak Table

Reproducing an
Arts and Crafts classic

by Victor J. Taylor

The lines of this sturdy table's rustic hayrake stretcher are reminiscent of the English farm tools and wagons that inspired its design.

An influential figure in the English Arts and Crafts movement around the turn of the century, Sidney Barnsley designed and made this massive oak table in 1924. Trained in London as an architect, Barnsley, along with his brother Ernest and their friend Ernest Gimson, was disenchanted with the impersonal, mass-produced furniture churned out by the machinery of the industrial age. So the three left urban life behind and retreated to the idyllic English countryside. In this peaceful setting they planned to make furniture that emphasized craftsmanship and integrity of design.

Sidney Barnsley was the loner of the trio. When differences arose among the three partners, he went his own way, hand-crafting all the pieces that came out of his workshop. His only machine was a large hand- and foot-powered circular saw.

Barnsley relied on his surroundings for many of his design ideas. Farm wagons and agricultural implements were common sights in the rural Cotswold hills of Gloucestershire where Barnsley set up his workshop. Their influence can be seen in this table's rustic "hayrake" stretcher—so called because its shape

resembles a type of wooden rake used in the fields. Barnsley used this design on many pieces and it became a sort of trade-mark. He also had a keen interest in Byzantine architecture, which is reflected in the chipcarving that decorates the top and legs of the table.

When reproducing this table, it's best to keep machining to a minimum. The parts may be cut out and surfaced by machine, but the beveling on the arrises of the top and legs and the chamfering on the stretcher and frame should be done by hand to keep the feel of the original.

Barnsley used English oak, but American red or white oak will work nicely. Three boards are edge-glued to make the top. The gluelines are reinforced with wedged butterfly keys (figure 1, detail B), also made from oak. Ideally, the boards used for the top should be quartersawn for stability; unfortunately, quartersawn oak is expensive and 1½-in. thick stock may be hard to find.

Make the butterfly keys before sawing out the sockets. Tilt the tablesaw blade 8°, and with four passes cut a 2-in. wide

Photo: Central Photographers, courtesy of Cheltenham Museum and Art Gallery

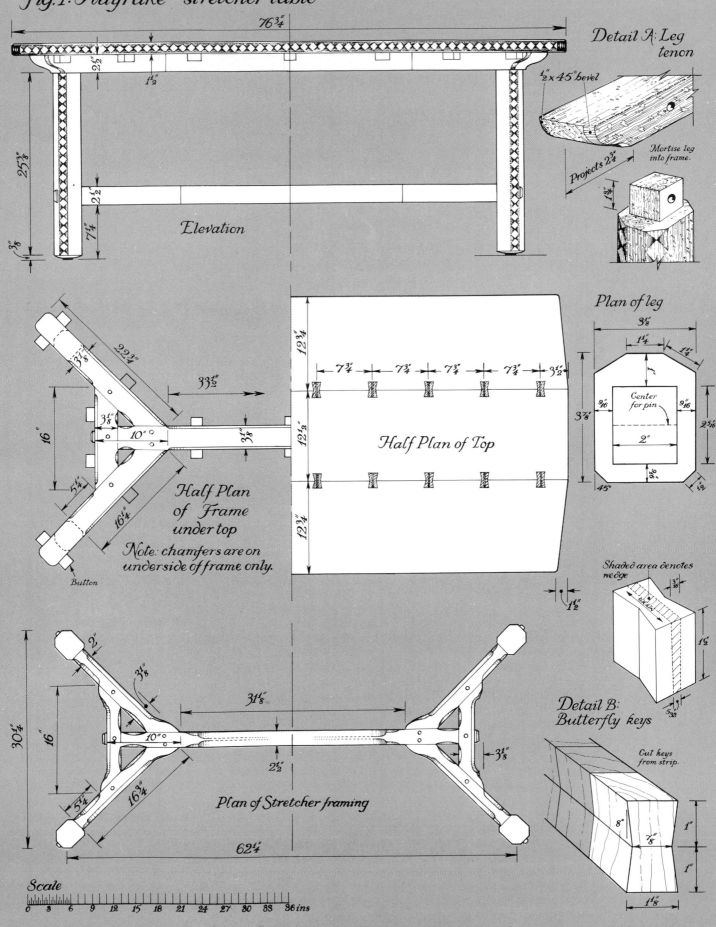

Fig. 1: Hayrake ~ stretcher table

76¾"

Detail A: Leg tenon

½" x 45° bevel

Mortise leg into frame.

Projects 2¾"

1⅜"

25⅜"

2½"

1½"

2½"

7¼"

⅜"

Elevation

Plan of leg

3⅝"

1¼"

1¼"

1"

Center for pin

9/16

9/16

3⅞"

2 5/16"

2"

9/16

45°

½"

3⅝"

22¾"

33½"

16"

3⅛"

10"

3⅛"

5¼"

16¼"

Half Plan of Frame under top

Note: chamfers are on underside of frame only.

Button

12¾"

7¾"   7¾"   7¾"   7¾"   3½"

12½"

Half Plan of Top

12¾"

1½"

Shaded area denotes wedge

grain

3/16"

1½"

5/32"

2"

3⅛"

31⅛"

30¾"

16"

10"

3⅛"

2½"

5¼"

16¼"

Detail B: Butterfly keys

Cut keys from strip.

8°

⅞"

1"

1"

1⅛"

Plan of Stretcher framing

62¼"

Scale

0 3 6 9 12 15 18 21 24 27 30 33 36 ins

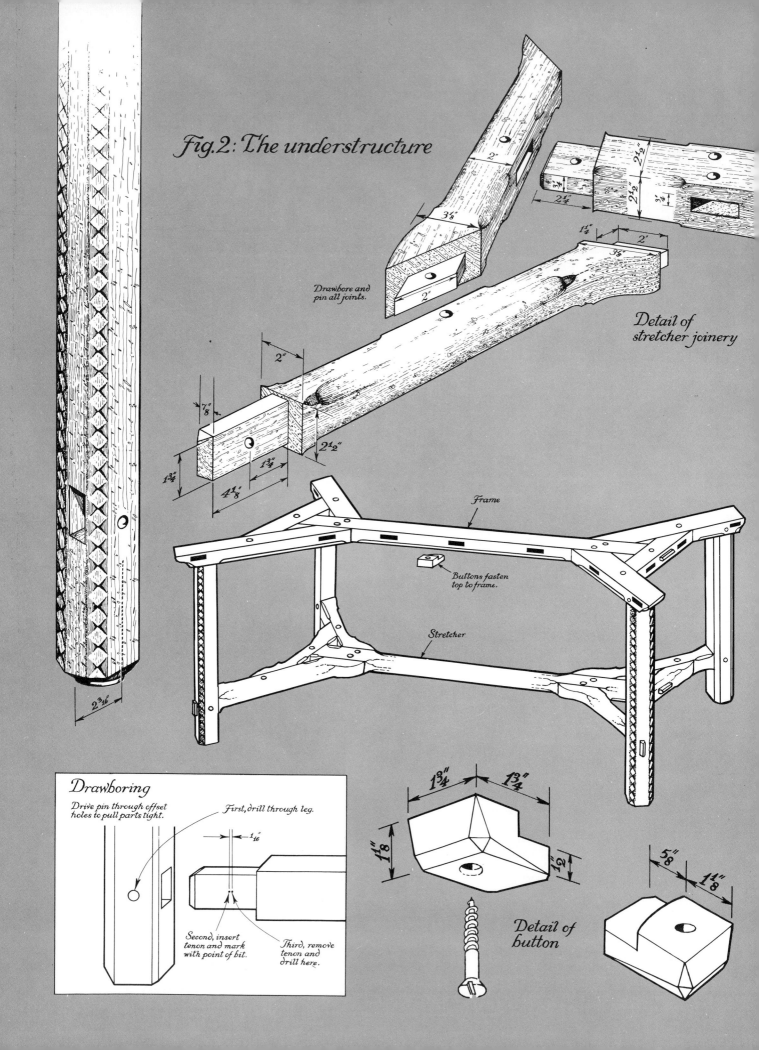

Fig.2: The understructure

Drawbore and
pin all joints.

2"

3⅜"

2½"

2¼"

2½"

2½"

¾"

8"

¾"

Detail of
stretcher joinery

1¼"

2'

3⅜"

2"

7/8"

1¾"

1¾"

4⅛"

2½"

Frame

Buttons fasten
top to frame.

Stretcher

2³⁄₁₆"

Drawboring

Drive pin through offset
holes to pull parts tight.

First, drill through leg.

1⁄16"

Second, insert
tenon and mark
with point of bit.

Third, remove
tenon and
drill here.

1¾"

1¾"

1⅛"

½"

Detail of
button

⅝"

1⅛"

crosscut section from a wide board to the butterfly shape, then cut individual keys off the strip. (If the grain runs in the right direction, you can use scraps from a wide, thick plank.) Instead of making a blind slot for the wedges, Barnsley sawed each key in half, then tapered the halves to match the wedge taper. Dry-assemble the tabletop and use each key as a template to mark out its socket. Unclamp the top and cut the sockets with a tenon saw, chiseling out the waste. The sockets go clear through the top.

Glue up the top and clamp lightly. Then glue the keys in their sockets. Insert the wedges end-grain-up and drive them home with a light tap from a mallet. When the wedges are all in place, tighten up the clamps.

Barnsley planed his tabletops by hand, and you might like to follow his example if you have energy to spare. Then angle off the ends of the top as shown in figure 1. Round off the corners with a block plane.

The dimensions and details for the hayrake stretcher are shown in figures 1 and 2. Cut the joints before shaping and rounding the parts. Barnsley used a timber-framing technique called drawboring to peg the joints. Holes for the ⅜-in. oak dowels are bored slightly out of line with each other. The distance between the hole centers need not be more than 1/16 in. When the pin is driven through, it draws the parts tightly together. This technique works best if the dowel is cut from green wood.

Shape the stretcher with a spokeshave and a drawknife. Use the spokeshave to start the chamfers at the corner, then continue with the drawknife. Push the spokeshave forward to create a gentle, curved lead-in to the main chamfering. The actual rounding off consists of a series of three separate chamfers. Although the stretcher appears round in cross section at its center, don't try to make a perfect circle. On the original table, the chamfered faces can still be felt by hand.

The top frame is similar to the stretcher, and the joinery is the same. There is no shaping or heavy chamfering on this assembly, but single chamfers are worked on the underside only. Chop mortises for the buttons that hold down the top. The legs are mortised into the underside of the top frame.

The chipcarving on the legs and edges of the top consists of shallow chisel cuts, as described in the box at right. Leave the work with a tool finish for a crisp, vigorous appearance.

It was impossible for me to discover what the original finish on the table was because the museum has been applying its own wax polish. The finish Barnsley used was probably a wax applied to the unfilled, unstained oak. I prefer a good-quality commercial wax polish, but you can make your own by shredding bleached beeswax and a smaller amount of carnauba wax into warm turpentine. Heat the mixture in a pan of hot water or on a radiator. Avoid open flames because the mixture is highly flammable. You've added enough wax when the mixture has a creamy consistency.

Before applying the wax, coat the wood with thinned shellac to seal the grain and prevent dirt and grime from getting into the pores. When the shellac is dry, apply the wax polish with a stiff-bristled brush. Brush in a generous amount, allow 24 hours for the turpentine to evaporate, then buff with a soft, lint-free cloth. The more you rub, the better the results will be. Apply several coats of wax at weekly intervals. □

Victor J. Taylor, an author and editor, lives in Bath, England. For more about Gimson and the Barnsleys, see Gimson and the Barnsleys *by Mary Comino (Van Nostrand Reinhold, 1982).*

Chipping away at decoration

The diamond chipcarving that ornaments Sidney Barnsley's hayrake table is one of the oldest forms of carving—and one of the easiest to master. The basic component of this and most other chipcarving is a triangular depression made by three cuts.

Make the first two cuts perpendicular to the work, deepest at the apex of the triangle and sloping to nothing where they join the third side. Hold the knife blade or chisel at a shallow angle to the work for the third cut, slicing from the base of the triangle down to the apex to pop up the chip. Repeat this sequence on the opposite side, and you have a diamond. That's all there is to it (well, almost).

Accurate layout is essential. Slight variations in the size of the squares won't be too noticeable, but errors can accumulate as the pattern repeats, and soon you won't have diamonds at all, just trapezoids. Draw the patterns directly on the wood with a sharp pencil, using a compass or a steel engineers' ruler to divide the surface into equal spaces.

For crisp detail, you should make each triangle by freeing one chip with only three cuts. But for large triangles, you may need to make the third cut in several steps, each removing a small chip until you've reached full depth. Too many cuts, however, and it will look like you nibbled the wood away.

Chipcarving is a pleasant way to whittle away idle hours and have something to show for it.   —V.J.T.

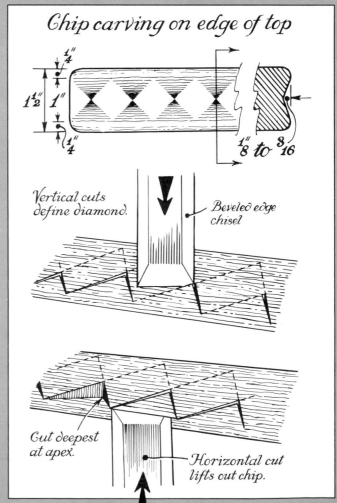

Chip carving on edge of top

1½"   1"

¼"

¼"

⅛" to 3/16"

Vertical cuts define diamond.

Beveled edge chisel

Cut deepest at apex.

Horizontal cut lifts out chip.

Working Locks Made of Wood
Though their security is symbolic, they're fun to make

by Roger Schroeder

Perhaps it is not so surprising that the first key-operated locks we know of, in use four thousand years ago, were made of wood. What is remarkable is that they operated on the principle of pins (called tumblers), the basic mechanisms of nearly all the locks we use today.

The notion of some kind of security device surely predates written or pictorial history. Lock experts surmise that the stone rolled in front of the cave was the first lock. It seems to me that this wouldn't have been much protection against an enemy stronger than the "locksmith." I suspect that the first lock was the wedge. Strategically placed, a wedge would have prevented the movement of a larger object, a tree trunk perhaps, that sheltered a small group of early men against their formidable, though less clever, enemies.

Many materials have been used for locks throughout history. The Gordian knot was a lock made from a single length of rope woven into an intricate pattern. Only those who knew its secret could pass through the gate and then retie the rope. As legend has it, Alexander the Great was confronted with the knot as a symbolic barrier to his invading army. He contemptuously slashed through it with a single blow from his sword, which of course anyone else could have done just as easily had they not been intimidated by the knot's implications. In the series that follows, locks 6, 8 and 9 historically were made of metal, but the wooden models illustrate the principles and would be just as functional as their metal prototypes in applications where their larger scale would be suitable. Any lock, even today, provides security that is more symbolic than real, for no lock can survive a concerted effort to break it. The presence of a lock has substantially the same effect as a sign saying "keep out." It is a barrier that, once crossed, brands the interloper as a criminal.

Locks on the Nile—It seems likely that as man became more social and agricultural, he invented devices for establishing barriers around his possessions, his family and his livestock. The first extensive use of wooden locks came at about the time the Egyptians entrenched themselves along the Nile, and the basic principles are still in use in Africa today, as shown in the photos of lock number 1 on the facing page. The typical Egyptian lock (above right) was made from teak. Massive in size, it had a bolt that measured 2 ft. to 3 ft. in length. This slid lengthwise through the lock to engage a staple (a U-shaped device attached to another door or to the door jamb).

Inside the lock were a number of slots arranged in an irregular pattern. Each slot contained a single pin-tumbler that could slide up and down freely. An enlarged head kept each pin from falling through. When the bolt slid into the staple, the wooden pins dropped into a matching set of holes in the upper face of the bolt, locking it in place.

To unlock the door, a curved key with a pattern of pegs

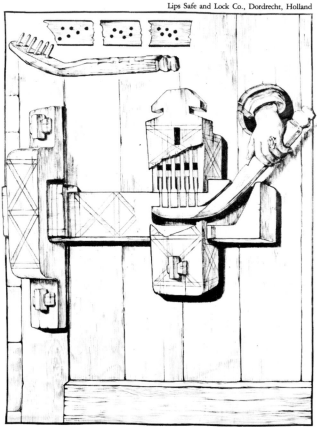

Lips Safe and Lock Co., Dordrecht, Holland

This Egyptian lock, in use 4,000 years ago, works on the same principles as the modern Moroccan lock (#1) shown on the facing page. Pegs on the key lift pins inside the lock to free the bolt.

that exactly matched the pattern of the tumbler holes was inserted into an opening in the bolt. When the key was raised, it pushed up the pin-tumblers until they cleared the bolt, which could then be slid sideways by pulling the key.

With as many as seven tumblers, the possible patterns would have numbered in the tens of thousands, but the thief of ancient Egypt, if he had the courage to stick his arm through the hole in the door, could coat a blank key with wax and raise it in the bolt. An impression would be left by the tumbler holes, showing him where to put pegs on his blank.

That this wooden lock should have originated in Egypt and not somewhere else does not surprise me. The pyramid builders had invented or made good use of many wooden devices, including the wedged mortise-and-tenon, the very means used for attaching their locks to doors.

This type of lock did not die with the ancient Egyptians. It was used in pre-Christian times by the Celts of Great Britain, who probably got it from the adventurous Phoenicians. Wooden locks of oak and yew were common in the Scottish Highlands well into the 19th century.

From *Fine Woodworking* magazine (September 1983) 42:60-65

1. Key-lifting today

The first lock I built, shown here, was modeled after one bought not long ago in a Moroccan market. It was sold as an operable hardware item. Instead of the bolt being hollowed, it is open at one end to allow the key with its pegs to be inserted. But the pin-tumblers and the collar that holds them are made as they were in ancient times.

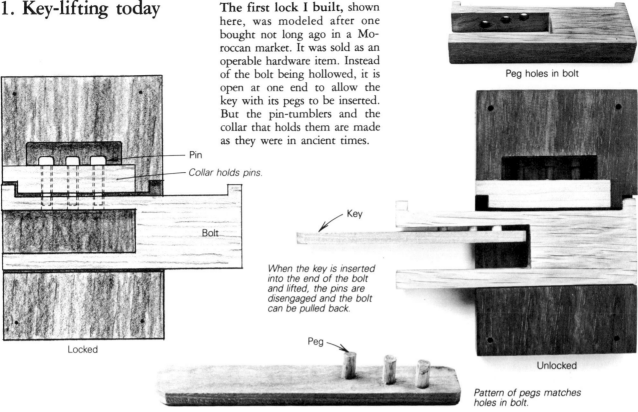

Peg holes in bolt

Pin

Collar holds pins.

Bolt

Key

When the key is inserted into the end of the bolt and lifted, the pins are disengaged and the bolt can be pulled back.

Peg

Locked

Unlocked

Pattern of pegs matches holes in bolt.

2. The Roman bit

Instead of pegs, the Roman key has bits, teeth-like projections that extend from its shank. When the key is raised, the bits lift the tumblers, which frees the bolt. Then the bolt can be slid back by means of a knob. Again, this type of wooden lock has not been relegated to ancient history; similar ones can be found in use today in parts of China, Egypt, Germany and the southern United States.

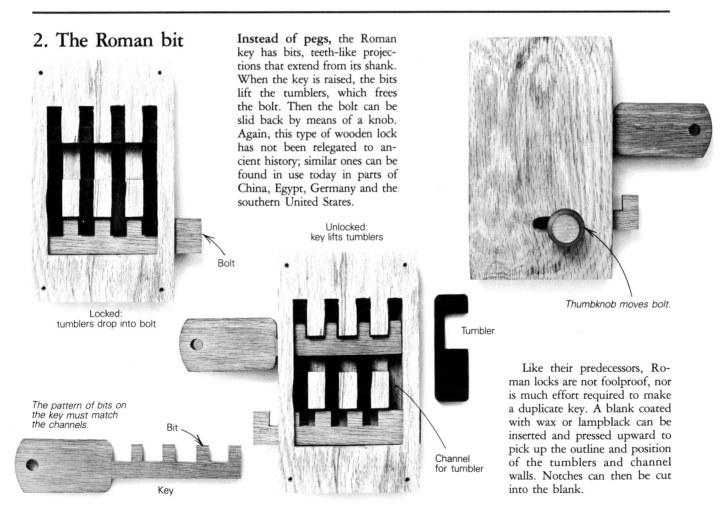

Locked:
tumblers drop into bolt

Bolt

Unlocked:
key lifts tumblers

Tumbler

Thumbknob moves bolt.

The pattern of bits on the key must match the channels.

Bit

Key

Channel
for tumbler

Like their predecessors, Roman locks are not foolproof, nor is much effort required to make a duplicate key. A blank coated with wax or lampblack can be inserted and pressed upward to pick up the outline and position of the tumblers and channel walls. Notches can then be cut into the blank.

3. Turning the key

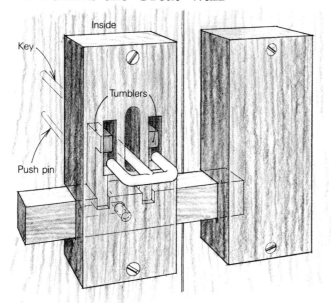

Bit

Key

Locked

Channel

Tumbler

Unlocked

Notch

When the lock is open, the key is trapped inside.

Pull end to retract bolt.

I built this model of a wooden lock found in an Egyptian ruin. This lock has a feature familiar to us—it requires a key that turns instead of lifts. When making the lock, care must be taken in cutting the notches in the tumblers so that the bits on the stem of the key can lift the tumblers smoothly upward without binding. To make the lock more difficult to pick, the bit sizes and their corresponding notches can be varied. Not visible in the photos is a device that keeps the bolt from being removed from the lock: a pin in a channel on the other side of the bolt.

A slight variation of this lock can be found today in China. The key is below the tumblers. When it is rotated, the bits push the tumblers upward, disengaging them from their notches in the bolt.

4. Behind the Great Wall

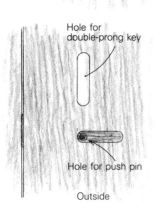

Inside

Key

Tumblers

Push pin

Hole for double-prong key

Hole for push pin

Outside

Another wooden lock extant in China uses a double-pronged iron key and pin, allowing the lock to be on the inside of the door, which makes the back of the lock inaccessible to intruders. The key is pushed through a vertical slot in the outside of the door, rotated 90°, and pulled forward so that the prongs engage the tumblers. When the key is lifted, the tumblers are raised from the bolt. A push pin rather than a thumbknob is used to slide the bolt to one side.

5. Easy unlock

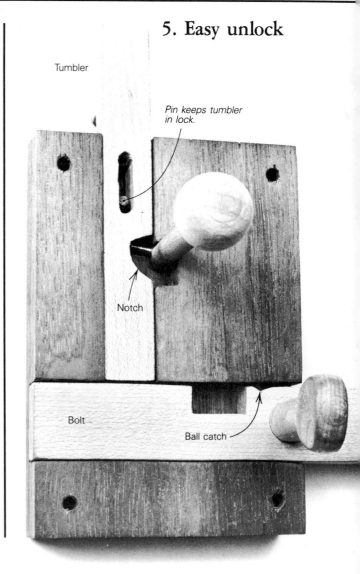

Tumbler

Pin keeps tumbler in lock.

Notch

Bolt

Ball catch

6. The warded lock

Key — Notch clears ward.

This lock is one-sided, but most warded locks are symmetrical, so that the key works from either side of the door.

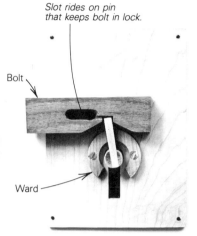

Slot rides on pin that keeps bolt in lock.

Bolt

Ward

Another Roman invention that remains in use after nearly two thousand years is the warded lock. Still found in older homes in the United States, this type of lock has an obstruction, called a ward, that prevents an alien key from turning in it. But a key that has the bit notched out so that it can pass the ward encounters the bolt and moves it. The shape of the keyhole can also act as a ward, as with our modern zigzag keys. But like the Egyptian lock and others, a warded lock is not very secure. A lockpicker can insert a blank covered with lampblack and turn it until it encounters a ward, which will leave a spot on the soot. The key can then be filed to shape. In locks with more than one ward, the lockpicker repeats the process until his bootleg key clears all the wards, opening the lock.

Key

Keyway

Bit

Thumbknob moves bolt.

A slight variation of these tumbler designs also puts the keyhole on the outside of the door. When the key (with a brass bit) is turned, a single tumbler is lifted and the bolt can be slid side-to-side with the aid of a thumbknob. This adaptation includes another improvement. The tumbler extends through the top of the lock, thereby making it possible to lock and unlock the door from the inside without the key. We take this for granted today, but this is the first lock design we have seen in this series that allows such an advantage.

When unlocked, a ball catch resists the bolt's movement, protecting it from being broken accidentally when the door is swung closed.

7. The spring lock

The Romans were the first to use another feature we take for granted today: springs. In keeping with the tradition of wooden locks, this simple one requires only a wedge-shaped wooden key to disengage the bolt. When the key is removed, the spring behind the bolt pushes it closed.

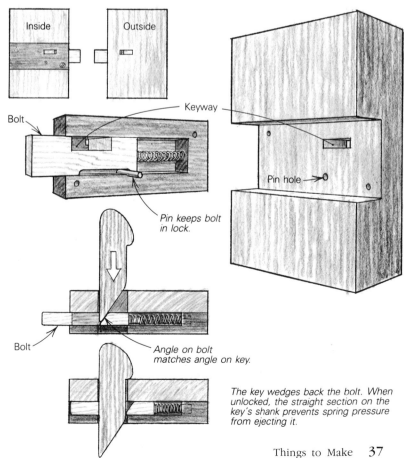

Inside

Outside

Bolt

Keyway

Pin hole

Pin keeps bolt in lock.

Bolt

Angle on bolt matches angle on key.

The key wedges back the bolt. When unlocked, the straight section on the key's shank prevents spring pressure from ejecting it.

8. The lever-tumbler

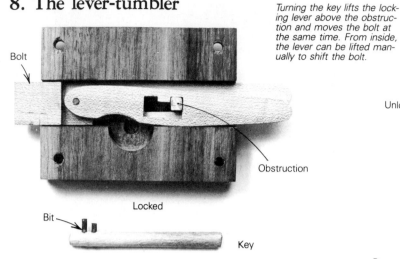

Bolt

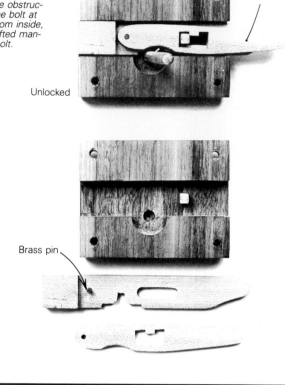

Lever

Unlocked

Turning the key lifts the locking lever above the obstruction and moves the bolt at the same time. From inside, the lever can be lifted manually to shift the bolt.

Obstruction

Locked

Bit

Key

Brass pin

The logical improvement of the warded lock, the lever-tumbler, is still in use today. Although it has a key with bits, it utilizes levers instead of pin-tumblers. One bit moves the bolt while another bit lifts a lever to free it. The security of this lock is in the number of levers used (sometimes ten) and in the size of the bits, which can be altered minutely, making it a more difficult lock to pick. This particular lock has two levers and operates with a key that has two brass pins for bits.

9. The Chinese combination

Keys, of course, can be lost, but the ancient Chinese came up with a solution—the combination lock. In remote times, as today, it could be opened only by correctly aligning letters or numbers on revolving rings. The one I built, similar to modern bicycle padlocks, has four rings numbered zero to nine. This means I have ten thousand possible combinations to choose from. And even though I committed myself to using four specific numbers when I permanently numbered the rings, I can still rearrange the numbered discs to change the combination. If I had used six rings, I would have had a million possible combinations, taxing my memory perhaps, but making lock-picking virtually impossible.

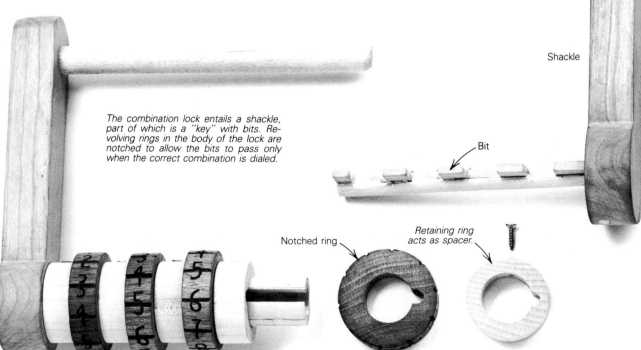

Shackle

The combination lock entails a shackle, part of which is a "key" with bits. Revolving rings in the body of the lock are notched to allow the bits to pass only when the correct combination is dialed.

Bit

Notched ring

Retaining ring acts as spacer.

10. Keyhole latch

Handle

Outside

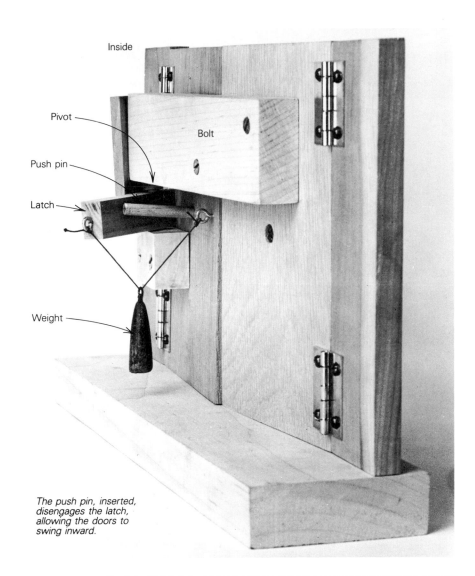

Inside

Pivot

Push pin

Latch

Weight

Bolt

The push pin, inserted, disengages the latch, allowing the doors to swing inward.

I built this wooden lock to scale from one found in Australia. Called a concealed lock, it has a bolt fastened to the inside of one door and held to the other by a wooden latch. The latch, which can pivot on a securely fastened base, has to be opened to release the bolt. The question is, how can the latch be pivoted from the outside? The secret of the lock is revealed by twisting the handle, which uncovers a hidden hole through which a push pin can be inserted. The string and weight are added so that when the doors are closed and the push pin removed, the latch will automatically close.

A modern pin-tumbler lock, cut away to reveal the works.

Locking it up—Though the Greeks are credited with inventing the all-important keyhole that eliminated the need to poke an arm through a hole in the door, their keys were large, shaped like sickles with wooden handles. The keys' security lay in the fact that they were metal, and individuals poor enough to want to steal did not have the price of the metal necessary for the key. It was the ingenious Romans, the first to use metal to make their locks, who made their keys small enough to be easily carried around.

Convenience seems to have been as important in the evolution of locks as any security they actually provided. The earliest wooden examples were bulky, clumsy, and (as we have seen) not too secure. Nevertheless, the designs are found in use today in such far-reaching places as the Congo, the East Indies, and the Alps, where huts are fitted with them. Wooden locks have survived despite their limitations because they have one advantage over iron and steel: in damp regions iron and steel rust tight, preventing the lock from functioning.

Yet the strength of metal has made the small contemporary lock possible. An interesting footnote is that one of our modern locks, patented just over a hundred years ago by Linus Yale, Jr., is a pin-tumbler lock much like the first Egyptian lock four millenia ago. Its major advantage over the Egyptian lock is the metal it is made from, pioneered by the Romans, who also introduced the other features that make it noteworthy—springs that hold its tumblers in position and the warded keyhole. With the Industrial Revolution in full swing, Mr. Yale was in the right milieu for innovation, but I wonder if he really thought he'd invented something new. □

Roger Schroeder, of Amityville, N.Y., is a woodworker and co-author of Woodcarving Illustrated. *He and* Fine Woodworking *magazine's Methods of Work editor, Jim Richey, made most of the locks shown here. Yes, they all work.*

Patternsawing
Identical pieces without much fuss

by Jim Cummins

When I bought an old building and moved my shop into it, I removed hundreds of square feet of wainscoting to make room for insulation and new electrical wiring. I used the salvageable pieces in refurbishing, but when the sheetrock and pegboard went up, I was left with innumerable splintery tongue-and-groove strips, which I sawed into short lengths to fit into my woodstove. When I finished, the pile filled one shop corner to the ceiling.

The first winter took care of only half the pile, but spring brought me an idea that would get rid of the rest, get my new shop some publicity, and raise a little money for the local guild of craftsmen besides. How? By patternsawing birdhouses, inviting the public to an open-house assembly party, and selling the birdhouses—one free to new guild members, $4 apiece otherwise.

The drawings show a few patternsawing setups for both the tablesaw and the bandsaw. With the appropriate setup, you can cut inside curves, outside curves, or in a straight line to produce exact multiples. These ideas aren't new, and most woodworkers will be familiar with at least one or two of them, but listing them together in this article may suggest even more possibilities.

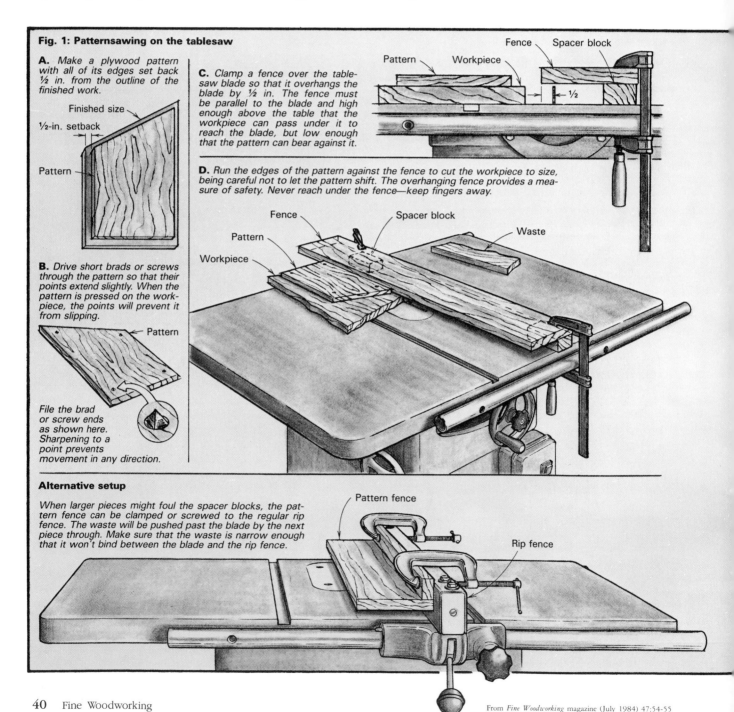

Fig. 1: Patternsawing on the tablesaw

A. *Make a plywood pattern with all of its edges set back ½ in. from the outline of the finished work.*

Finished size
½-in. setback
Pattern

B. *Drive short brads or screws through the pattern so that their points extend slightly. When the pattern is pressed on the workpiece, the points will prevent it from slipping.*

Pattern

File the brad or screw ends as shown here. Sharpening to a point prevents movement in any direction.

C. *Clamp a fence over the tablesaw blade so that it overhangs the blade by ½ in. The fence must be parallel to the blade and high enough above the table that the workpiece can pass under it to reach the blade, but low enough that the pattern can bear against it.*

D. *Run the edges of the pattern against the fence to cut the workpiece to size, being careful not to let the pattern shift. The overhanging fence provides a measure of safety. Never reach under the fence—keep fingers away.*

Pattern   Workpiece   Fence   Spacer block
½

Fence   Spacer block   Waste
Pattern
Workpiece

Alternative setup

When larger pieces might foul the spacer blocks, the pattern fence can be clamped or screwed to the regular rip fence. The waste will be pushed past the blade by the next piece through. Make sure that the waste is narrow enough that it won't bind between the blade and the rip fence.

Pattern fence
Rip fence

From *Fine Woodworking* magazine (July 1984) 47:54-55

In each setup, the workpiece is fastened to a pattern that controls the line of the cut by bearing against a fence—you don't have to eyeball curved cuts and you don't have to change fence adjustments to make straight cuts of various widths or at various angles. The reference edges are on the pattern, which means that you can saw irregular scraps to size with the first cut, without initially having to establish clean edges to run against the fence.

The pattern and the workpiece usually are held together by something like nails, brads or sharpened screw points driven through the pattern so that their tips protrude just enough to catch the workpiece and hold it flat. With this method, there's no slow jigging and clamping from one workpiece to the next, which is an advantage over other production setups. In my case, I just lined up a couple of pieces of wainscoting side-by-side on the saw table, and pressed the tongue and groove together. Then I could slap the pattern on top, which automatically held things in place, and cut the work to size without having to do a lot of extra trimming. Instead of driving brads through the pattern to keep the work from shifting, I covered the entire bottom of the pattern with non-slip rubber tape. You could use sandpaper, too, but I wouldn't recommend either of these methods for very large pieces.

Patternsawing worked great in my shop. Over the course of about five hours, we made 54 birdhouses, recruited 22 new guild boosters, and raised about $120 in cash for the guild. As a bonus, I had beady-eyed, perky little wrens outside my bedroom window all summer long. I watched four little birds grow up and fly away, and never had to set my alarm clock once until September. □

Jim Cummins is an associate editor at Fine Woodworking.

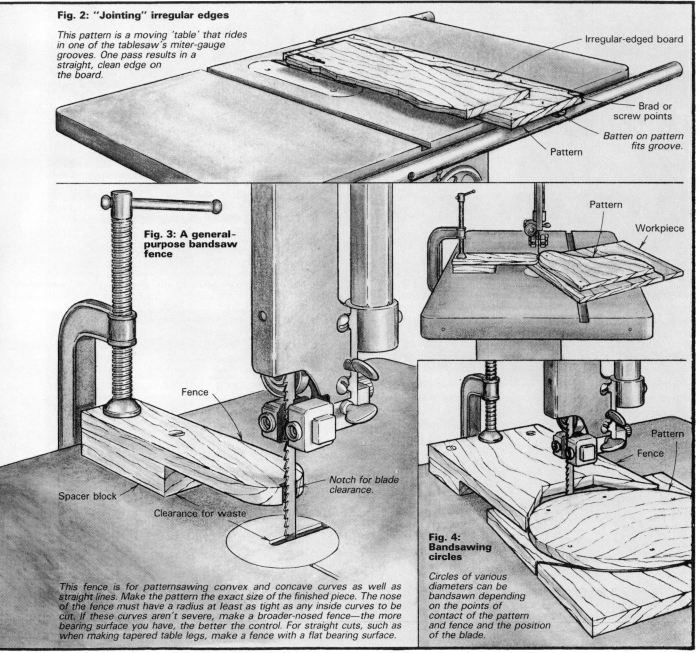

Fig. 2: "Jointing" irregular edges
This pattern is a moving 'table' that rides in one of the tablesaw's miter-gauge grooves. One pass results in a straight, clean edge on the board.

Irregular-edged board

Brad or screw points

Batten on pattern fits groove.

Pattern

Fig. 3: A general-purpose bandsaw fence

Fence

Notch for blade clearance.

Spacer block

Clearance for waste

This fence is for patternsawing convex and concave curves as well as straight lines. Make the pattern the exact size of the finished piece. The nose of the fence must have a radius at least as tight as any inside curves to be cut. If these curves aren't severe, make a broader-nosed fence—the more bearing surface you have, the better the control. For straight cuts, such as when making tapered table legs, make a fence with a flat bearing surface.

Pattern

Workpiece

Pattern

Fence

Fig. 4: Bandsawing circles

Circles of various diameters can be bandsawn depending on the points of contact of the pattern and fence and the position of the blade.

ure out the width, so I went back to my pencil and paper to make a real scale drawing. I could tell from looking through Janet's triangle that it was best to keep reality to a minimum in this object; that is, the open space you look through shouldn't be very big. I chose ⅜ in. for the inside width of the strips and set up a fence on the saw. I left figuring out the size of the glass until later. Always leave the hard stuff until later.

I cut all my odds and ends of pretty wood into long strips with the proper angle on their edges to make a hexagon (60°), then I had to think about the glass. It wasn't that hard to figure out on the drawing, but I knew the reality of cutting the mirror strips would be different. If the glass came out a touch too big, the kaleidoscope might not assemble at all; if it was too small, gaps would show. I couldn't see any way to build in a com-

Six mirrored strips, stuck to a masking tape clamp, fold up into a kaleidoscope.

fortable margin of error, so I went for "just right."

I didn't cut a zillion strips of glass, not right then. I wanted a prototype. I figured that the glass strips needed to be a smidgen more than ¼ in. wide and 3¾ in. long. I wanted the kaleidoscope to be 4 in. long, to keep it in proportion with its diameter, and so it would fit in a shirt pocket.

I cut six strips of mirror tile, the cheapest sort of mirror there is. Then I crosscut all the long strips of wood to 4-in. lengths. Even though it was prototype time, once the saw was set up for that length I wasn't going to take any chances of anything changing.

Now it was time to assemble the prototype. I went right to it in that exalted

creative state where nothing, not supper, not war, not love, could interfere with *finishing the first kaleidoscope.* I had read in *Fine Woodworking* about clamping miters with masking tape, and I was anxious to try it. I laid out six strips and put masking tape on their backs, leaving enough overhang to tape the last joint. Then I turned the whole thing over and contact-cemented the bits of mirror to the wood.

I had only to clean the glass and I was ready for assembly—how quickly this project was going! I knew from experience that Windex wouldn't remove contact cement, so I swabbed down the glass with kerosene (my all-purpose cleaner) and wiped it off.

To assemble the kaleidoscope, I squirted a thin bead of white glue into each joint, rolled the thing up and stuck down the tape overhang to hold the last joint tight. The glass grated a bit, but settled into place with the help of some judicious hand pressure. Then I went and made myself a cup of coffee and waited for the glue to dry. I was pretty excited.

Ten minutes before I could reasonably have expected the glue to be dry, I peeled off the tape. The kaleidoscope held together okay. I peered in and saw the reality hexagon in the end—not too obtrusive. Around that was a ring of perfect hexagons, and an exciting world of long strips and shadow hexagons reaching all the way to my eye. I'd made magic out of wood and glass and tape and glue.

I trued the ragged ends of the hexagon on the disc sander. The neat little hexagon miters were nice, but they looked unfinished, so I thought I'd better stick on end pieces, with holes in them to look through: I drilled some trial holes in ¼-in. stock to get the size. It was obvious that to see hexagons, which I liked seeing, the hole had to be bigger than all of the glass—⁹⁄₁₆ in. in this case. And if the hole intruded at all on the glass, I got circles, which were kind of nice, too. So I decided to put a ⁷⁄₁₆-in. hole on the other end. Now I could see hexagons through one end and circles through the other.

It occurred to me that kaleidoscopes might not come in under $5, and might in fact be more finicky work than they were worth. But I was hooked enough to plunge ahead. I rushed to the hardware store, which was just closing, and got a ⁷⁄₁₆-in.-twist drill. "Charge it!" I cried, and raced back to the shop to make some kaleidoscope end pieces.

I couldn't imagine *clamping* all those end pieces, and speedy cyanoacrylate glue

doesn't work well on end grain, so I opted for contact cement. It was already out on the bench anyway. Besides, it's important to center the end pieces properly, and contact cement is just the thing. I brushed it on, waited a few minutes, fidgeting, then peered through while aiming the end piece. When the piece was just right, I clapped it on and squeezed it a moment with my fingers (to be safe, you could also snug it up in the vise).

I lopped off the overhanging corners of the end piece on the bandsaw, then sanded the kaleidoscope smooth on my stationary belt sander, using all the usual bag of tricks—rolling the corners over to get them a bit round, nicking off the sharp end points, and so on. It didn't take long. The kaleidoscope was a nice, smooth, heavy little thing to hold in your hand. I pulled a rag through to get out the sanding dust, gave the thing a rub with 220-grit garnet paper, and put on some oil to finish it up. I was captivated anew, and popped it in my shirt pocket to show people.

That first generation of kaleidoscopes was pretty nice, but when they were all done, I had time for a breather and a bit of thinking. As you can see from the photo on p. 46, I decided to switch from a six-sided configuration to a five-sided one (where the strip angle is 54°), for less symmetry and a bit more speed, and I cleaned up a few details that had been bothering me, like making the whole gadget 4¼ in. long so the mirrors could be 4 in. and I could get three of them out of a 12-in. mirror tile with no trimming. These things matter to the short-run production woodworker, who must live in a world of stolen seconds. I also got the glass to work out so it was exactly ⁵⁄₁₆ in. wide, instead of "a smidgen more than ¼ in." If you're going to make several hundred of something, it ought to be truly repeatable.

I like this product because it appeals to just about everybody. It really is sort of fun to have one in your shirt pocket so you can take it out and look at things that way, for a little while, if you want to.

Price? Well, it didn't get in under $5. It looks like it's worth more than that anyway, being sort of heavy and complicated and made out of wood. I charge $9 for them (1985). I think they'd even sell for $10. It's not the "Grail," but it's a nice little thing to make.   □

Robin Kelsey makes his living doing short-run production woodworking in Maynooth, Ont.

Project: Music Stand

by John D. Freeman

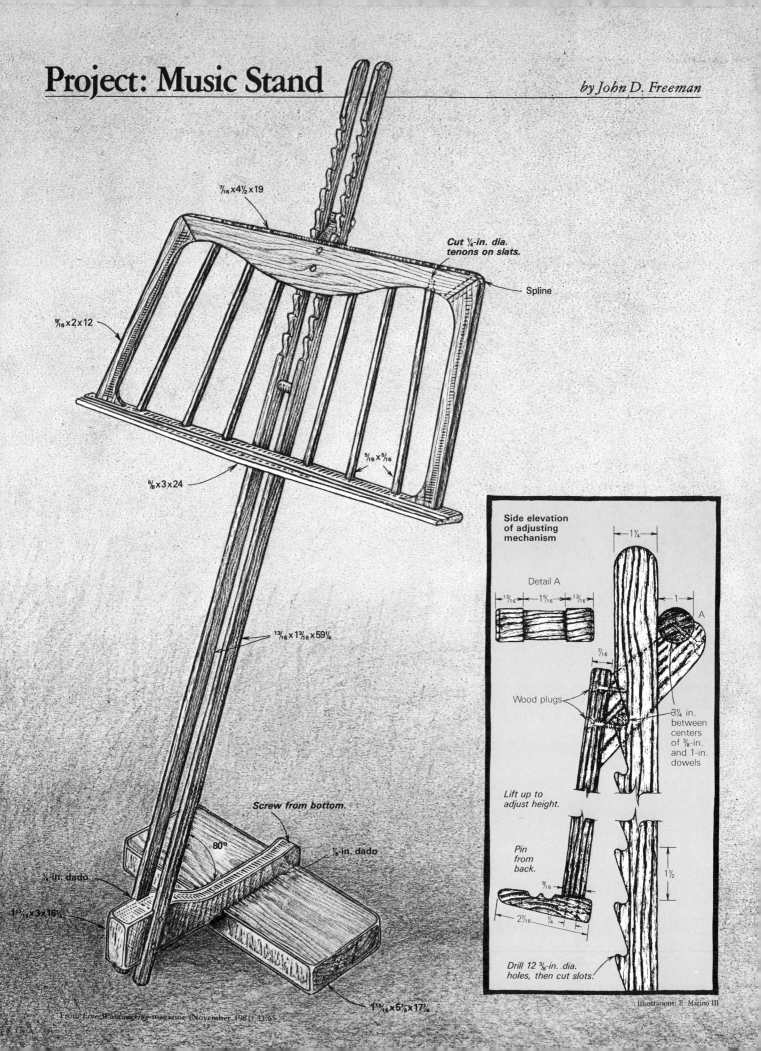

⁷⁄₁₆ x 4½ x 19

Cut ¼-in. dia. tenons on slats.

Spline

⁹⁄₁₆ x 2 x 12

⁵⁄₁₆ x ⁵⁄₁₆

⅝ x 3 x 24

¹³⁄₁₆ x 1¾₆ x 59¼

Screw from bottom.

80°

⅛-in. dado

¼ in. dado

1¹³⁄₁₆ x 3 x 15¾

1¹³⁄₁₆ x 5⅝ x 17¾

Side elevation of adjusting mechanism

1¼

Detail A

¹³⁄₁₆ 1⁵⁄₁₆ ¹³⁄₁₆

1

⁷⁄₁₆

A

Wood plugs

3¼ in. between centers of ⅜-in. and 1-in. dowels

Lift up to adjust height.

Pin from back.

⁹⁄₁₆

2⁷⁄₁₆   ¼

1½

Drill 12 ⅜-in. dia. holes, then cut slots.

Illustrations: E. Marino III

From Fine Woodworking magazine (November 1981) 31-65.

The American Harp
Ancient form, steel strings

by Robert T. Cole

Crossbar

Tuning pegs

f-hole

Nut

Bridge

Neck

Ring

End pins

Top plate

Butt plate

Tuning beads

Bottom plate

The lyre form of the harp is the most ancient of stringed instruments, and it has evolved into a variety of forms. I designed the instrument here to be used with high-tension steel strings; it is strong and stable, and it includes carved front and back plates. No other lyres have been built like this, so I call this the American harp. Regardless of the name, its function, as usual, is to encourage music at home and singing in particular. It can be tuned to many scales, so there's enough complexity to occupy the player for years.

Materials
1½ x 10 x 16 Philippine or
Honduras mahogany
¾ x 10 x 20 Philippine or
Honduras mahogany
1½ x 2 x 5 hardwood crossbar
Hardwood strips for nut,
bridge and butt plate
¼-in. dowel, 10 in. long
Wooden beads (8)
Piano-tuner's pegs (8)
Guitar strings (8)
Guitar end pins (8)—you can
make your own

The ring, shown in the drawing at right, forms the sides and necks of the harp. It may be cut out on a bandsaw or with a coping saw. It is then cleaned up using both a disc sander and a drum sander. The overall width of the harp may vary between 9½ in. and 10 in., and the thickness of the wall ranges from ¼ in. on the sides to ⅝ in. where the end pins will be drilled. Do not round any edges until the harp is glued up.

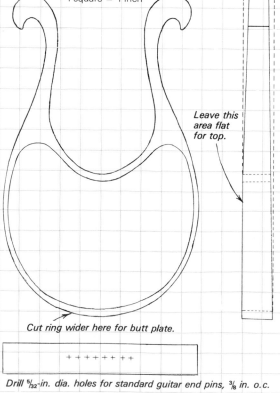

1 square = 1 inch

Leave this area flat for top.

Cut ring wider here for butt plate.

+ + + + + + + +

Drill ⁵⁄₃₂-in. dia. holes for standard guitar end pins, ³⁄₈ in. o.c.

Drawings: E. Marino III

The crossbar should be made from a strong hardwood, like maple, oak or koa. Trace the inside curve of the necks onto the crossbar blank, then cut and shape it to fit. Bevel its two faces, and drill holes for the tuning pegs slightly smaller than the pegs. Tuning pegs can be had from a piano supply house, and a tap-wrench handle works well to adjust them. Glue in the crossbar, and when dry, drill and pin it with four ¼-in. dowels.

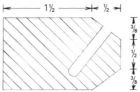

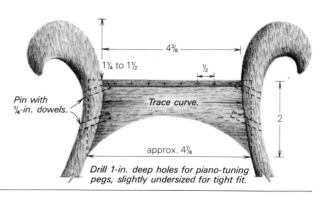

Pin with ¼-in. dowels.

Trace curve.

approx. 4⅞

Drill 1-in. deep holes for piano-tuning pegs, slightly undersized for tight fit.

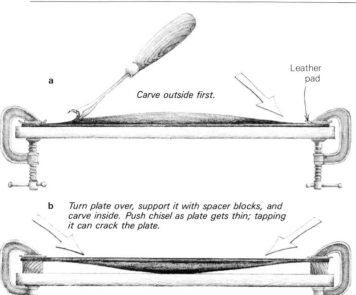

a — Carve outside first.

Leather pad

b — Turn plate over, support it with spacer blocks, and carve inside. Push chisel as plate gets thin; tapping it can crack the plate.

c — Add brace under bridge position, if needed.

⅛ to 3/32

Slightly thinner here

Now you can carve the plates. First saw the outline from the ¾-in. thick mahogany blank, leaving ⅛-in. trim. Clamp the blank to the bench, outside up, and fair the edges with a wide gouge (a). Turn the blank over, clamp it to the bench using spacer blocks, and begin carving the inside face (b). As the plate gets thin, push the chisel rather than tap it (or use a disk grinder), or you risk splitting the wood. Quite often you must unclamp and feel its thickness. It should approach 3/32 in. near where it will be glued. If it deflects more than 1/16 in. under moderate pressure, you should add a brace under where the bridge will be (c). If you carve the plate too thin at any spot, glue on a wood patch.

Smooth the inside with sandpaper and refine the contour, Then cut the *f*-holes in the top plate—carefully, as it is easy to split the thin wood (d). Next cut out the space for the butt plate. This is where the strings will lay over the end, and they would cut through the softer mahogany.

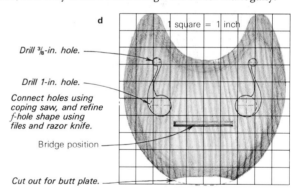

d

1 square = 1 inch

Drill ⅜-in. hole.

Drill 1-in. hole.

Connect holes using coping saw, and refine *f*-hole shape using files and razor knife.

Bridge position

Cut out for butt plate.

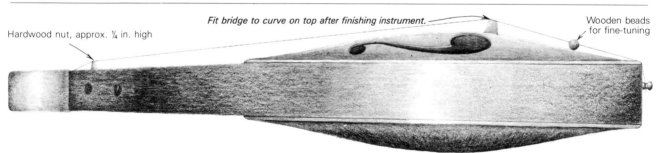

Fit bridge to curve on top after finishing instrument.

Hardwood nut, approx. ¼ in. high

Wooden beads for fine-tuning

Glue up one plate at a time, back, then front, checking first to see that the surfaces make good contact. I use aliphatic resin (yellow) glue and clamp with C-clamps every couple of inches, protecting the wood with leather pads. When the front plate is dry, glue on the butt plate and drill the end-pin holes. Round all the edges and finish-sand.

Make the hardwood nut about ¼ in. high and glue it to the crossbar. I finish the harp now using a brushing lacquer—three coats, sanding between

coats and rubbing with steel wool at the end. Now fit the bridge to the curve of the top and slot it for the strings: Use regular guitar strings, as shown:

String	Tuning
0.046 wound	Bass C
0.036 wound	G
0.026 wound	C ′
0.020 wound	E
0.016 plain	G ′
0.012 plain	C ″
0.010 plain	E ′
0.008 plain	G ″

Other tunings are possible. Bring all the strings up to tension, then fine-tune using the wooden beads between the end pins and the bridge. The first tuning takes patience because the instrument needs to adjust to the tension.

The harp can be played by plucking, or with hammer-dulcimer sticks made of felt, to produce the effect of a steel-string lyrical drum. ☐

Robert Cole, of Santa Barbara, Calif., is a luthier.

From *Fine Woodworking* magazine (November 1981) 31:70-71

The Appalachian Dulcimer
How Warren May makes traditional instruments

by Billy F. Best

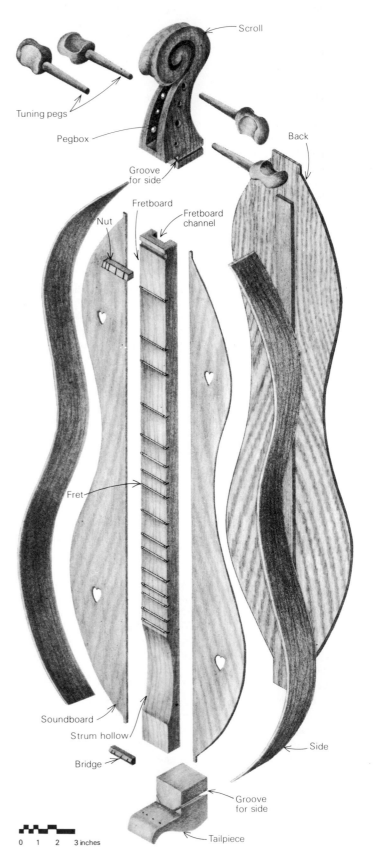

Tuning pegs

Scroll

Pegbox

Back

Groove for side

Fretboard

Fretboard channel

Nut

Fret

Soundboard

Strum hollow

Bridge

Side

Groove for side

Tailpiece

0 1 2 3 inches

Visitors walking past the Upstairs Gallery in Berea, Ky., are likely to hear dulcimer music. The player, and the instrument maker, is Warren A. May, who has been making dulcimers for nine years. Because there is no definitive standard, dulcimers tend to be one-of-a-kind projects that allow the maker to take advantage of available sizes of wood, and to vary the overall shape, the decorative scroll carving, the shape of the sound holes, and even the number of strings. Four years ago, when he was making instruments at the rate of two per week, May realized that certain shapes and sizes no longer varied from one to the next. He'd settled the length of the fretboard and its fret spacing, the shape and size of the pegbox, scroll, and tailpiece. Why, he asked himself, was he still making these parts one at a time?

By applying production techniques, jigs, and time-saving ingenuity, he figured he could make more, and better, dulcimers. May will make about 400 instruments this year, yet finds he has more time to make music as well. By building around a standard framework (composed of pegbox, tailpiece, and fretboard), and by making multiples of only those other parts of the instrument that don't change, May frees himself from routine tasks, finds time to search out unusually figured wood, and can custom-build body shapes to suit individual customers' preferences. If he has a fine piece of spruce a little wider than usual, he won't cut away good wood, he'll just make a wide dulcimer.

What follows are some of the ways May has improved both the production and the musical quality of his instruments, without compromising his freedom to design.

May has established a straightforward routine for pegboxes: He squares up the stock, bandsaws the rough shape, and tablesaws the tapers. He drills out the channel with a Forstner bit, then forms the scroll with a router-equipped pantograph. Then he rounds the edges with a router, flap-sands, and takes his time carving the finishing touches with a penknife.

Cutting the grooves for the frets is an exacting job. They have to be correctly spaced, or the instrument won't play in tune. They have to be the right depth and width, else the fret-wire inserts won't fit properly. Instead of cutting the grooves one at a time, May uses a home-made gang-saw based on pillow blocks, with a sliding table made with drawer glides (photo, facing page). A saw-sharpening shop ground the teeth of the inexpensive 4-in. blades (from Sears) to make a 0.020-in. kerf for the fret wire. The next time he changes blades ("It only runs four hours a year..."), May plans to use industrial quality. One extra-thick blade cuts the groove for the nut. This rig can saw two fretboards per minute. May channels the underside of the fretboard as far as the strum hollow with a dado saw. Then he shapes the strum hollow with a bandsaw and a standing belt sander.

Any bandsaw would do to make the tops, backs, and sides, but May converted a 3-HP meat bandsaw that lets him deal

From *Fine Woodworking* magazine (March 1982) 33:68-70

with difficult woods (like the poplar timbers he salvaged from a 100-year-old house in town) without bogging down.

Instead of beading the overhanging edges of the top and back with scrapers and carving tools, a 45-minute job that risked catching grain, or slipping and drawing blood, May uses a Dremel tool as a router. The sharpening shop re-ground a carbide router bit to May's design. Then May had the shank turned to fit the Dremel. Now the beading takes four minutes, and even a curly maple top is no problem.

May has abandoned full-instrument jigs. He feels that he gets better joints by free-clamping the parts of the instrument. This method allows him to vary body shapes easily, even though the length of the instruments remains the same.

May glues the two pieces of the soundboard to the channeled fretboard, forming a stiff, hollow-bottomed assembly. He bookmatches the back by jointing the glueline, taping the pieces together on the outside, and setting them up on the bench like a shallow tent, with the tape on the bottom. They are held in position by nails around the edges. When the tent is pressed flat by a weighted board, the nails spring the joint tight. This works with any size board and any irregular shape. When the top-assembly, back, pegbox and tailpiece are glued together, they form an open-sided framework.

The bookmatched sides are all the same depth and thickness because they must fit the standard grooves in the pegbox and tailpiece, but their length can vary according to the size and shape of the body. May soaks and overbends each side on an adjustable form made from a piece of plywood with dowels inserted to hold the sides upright. Finishing nails (covered with plastic straws to protect the wood from stains) are driven into the plywood to outline the shape. The exact shape isn't critical. May inserts one end in the tailpiece groove, then clamps and glues his way toward the pegbox, wiggling-in the bent sides as he goes. He clamps them in place

Glue.

Two clothespins, filler piece and bicycle inner tube

with spring clamps which he alternates with clothespin clamps he makes in his shop (left). When he gets near the pegbox, he estimates the length needed to fill the groove, cuts off the waste, and slips the side into place. This operation determines the final shape and the strength of the finished instrument, so May takes his time here, averaging about ten minutes per side.

May has found that innumerable glue blocks around the sides are unnecessary, so he uses them only at points where the side is liable to spring in during glue-up. He uses interior bracing only around sound holes (where edges might catch on clothing), and in extra-wide instruments where he feels the back is bound to bow. "If they'd bow out," he says, "it would be all right, but when they bow in, they look terrible."

He chooses not to use lining around the inside. He finds it unnecessary for strength, and the absence of it frees the soundboard for easier, more responsive vibration. "Overbuilt instruments," he says, "can sound clunky."

Tuning pegs and their corresponding holes in the pegbox are tapered to a wedge fit, so the string will hold its tune. May rough-turns his rosewood pegs (keys) and trues the tapers with a violinmakers' matched reamer and peg-cutter set, assuring smooth tuning. The set costs $50 (1982), but it speeds the work and assures uniform tuning on every instrument.

May uses two coats of sealer and two of lacquer on each dul-

Warren May details the scroll of a dulcimer with a penknife, after a series of jigs and machines have produced the basic shape.

May's gang-saw, above, is a shaft running in pillow blocks, with blades ground to the width of the fret wire. The top is a sliding table made from plywood and drawer glides. Different-sized inserts can adjust the spacing of the blades. One pass will make all the cuts on May's standard fretboard, guaranteeing uniformity and accuracy. Below, May dry-clamps the framework, which is composed of the tailpiece, back, pegbox, and the fretboard-top subassembly. He wiggles-in the sides after the framework has been glued up. The plane merely steadies the pieces while May sets the clamps.

cimer. The second coat of lacquer can dry too glossy, out of place on a traditional instrument, but still a finish is necessary to protect the wood. May's solution is to polish the final coat with 0000 steel wool, using paste wax as a lubricant, which quickly produces a smooth, satin glow.

He uses yellow glue for most joints, and high-resin white glue for the sides, instead of the tricky (he says "undependable") hide glues that most instrument makers use. When it was pointed out to him that this would make the instruments harder to take apart for repair, May countered: "What repairs? I don't anticipate any. I've never had a joint come open, and there's nothing inside to come loose. My instruments all have a lifetime guarantee." □

Bill Best runs the Upward Bound program at Berea College in Ky. Photos by Steven Bradford.

How a dulcimer makes music

A stringed instrument without the refinements is just a box that you can't open. Here are some of the details May has noted after years developing his traditional dulcimer design.

May uses five woods. His favorite dulcimers are made with quartersawn spruce for the top, and cherry for the back and sides. He likes the combination of volume (from the cherry) and tone (the spruce). When he builds an instrument from one wood, he'll use sapwood or lighter textured wood for the top, heartwood for the back and sides. The lighter wood responds to the string vibration, and the heartwood reflects the sound and resists the dampening effect of the player's body. He says walnut is the customers' general favorite, because it has a smoother sound than cherry, which he likes for its brightness. Curly maple has a smaller sound than cherry, but it's clean and crisp. Mahogany and poplar are his other standards. If you mix woods at random, May cautions, you can end up with an unmusical, hard-to-tune instrument.

When May uses a hard wood like curly maple for the top, he reduces its thickness so it will respond more easily to the strings. His tops are usually ³/₃₂ in. thick, as are the backs and sides.

By channeling the fretboard, it is lightened (allowing the string vibration to pass through) without losing stiffness. The narrow gluing area also allows the top to vibrate freely. If you don't use a lining around the sides, you don't have to worry about binding and purfling to restore the top's responsiveness at the outside edges.

String weight determines ease of playing and volume. May uses a bass string of wound 0.022-ga. steel, and three top strings of 0.012-ga. plain steel; guitar and banjo strings work

This teardrop-shaped dulcimer, based on the standard framework, takes advantage of an unusual piece of wood with naturally-formed soundholes. Photo: Frank Hudson.

fine. The strings are tuned G-G-G-C. The two bottom strings (farthest from the player's body) are drones, sometimes chorded. The melody is played on the top strings in unison. Notes are fretted with the fingers, or with a "noter," a stick used to press down the strings.

May plays his music in the traditional Appalachian style. He grew up in a log cabin with nine brothers and sisters, and has learned to play so well that the sound of his music pulls passersby into his Upstairs Gallery, in Berea. Although he's familiar with some of the other directions dulcimers can take (different bridge placements, soundposts, more frets) he feels that these distort the natural dulcimer sound and harmony.

He strums his instruments high up on the fretboard, close to his fretting hand. There's a reason for this style: since the string vibration travels to the soundboard at both ends (because of the construction of the instrument), the closer to the middle you strike the string, the purer the tone. When you use a pick, though, you play over the strum hollow, so you don't scratch the fretboard.

Pegbox design is trickier than it looks, because the strings must clear the wood as well as each other, otherwise tuning is an uncertain chore.

The length of each string determines its pitch. You can choose spacings for the tempered scale used on pianos and guitars, which averages out the correct spacings for different musical modes, or you can choose one mode in favor of the

others. May has settled on Ionian mode spacing as the best suited to his kind of dulcimer music. This spacing is shown at the bottom of this page.

String height depends on the depth of the notches in the nut and bridge. The important thing to keep in mind is that if strings are too high, they'll hurt your fingers, and if they're too low, they'll buzz on the frets. The nut should keep the unstopped strings as low as possible without allowing buzzing (file the notch too deep, though, and you need a new nut), and the bridge should be high enough to keep the strings about ³/₁₆ in. above the bottom fret. Frets can be adjusted and trued with a file so they're even.

The bridge floats on the fretboard; thus you can cant it down on one side (the bass strings are made longer) to keep the different weight strings in tune.

When you evaluate a dulcimer, remember that performers may look for volume and carrying power, but the average player wants a more intimate character. May recommends that you try out an instrument in a room like the one you'll play it in, or you won't hear its true sound. —B.F.B.

For more fine-tuning and different points of view, read Foxfire 3 *(New York: Doubleday, 1975); Hines,* How to make and play the Dulcimore *(Harrisburg, Pa.: Stackpole Books, 1973); and Harris,* Notes on Dulcimer Making *(Okla. City: Bois D'Arc, 1977).*

Fret spacing for the Ionian mode—overall length of this fretboard is 27½ in.

Floating bridge

Nut

Q & A

Building a violin case—*I'm building a violin case with an arched lid. I would like to use plywood for the top panel, but I'm not sure how I can bend it. Would I have to glue up veneers on a form, or could I simply bend a piece of Baltic birch plywood? I would also like to know what's the best way to attach the arch to a solid wood frame.*
—*David Pinals, Belmont, Mass.*

ROBERT MEADOW REPLIES: I recommend that you use ⅛-in. Italian poplar bending plywood for the top, rather than the Baltic birch plywood. The birch is too stiff, and the poplar will give you a better surface on which to glue the leatherette covering. To avoid the chore of mold-building at The Luthierie, our instrument-making and woodworking school in Saugerties, N.Y., we use bending irons, but if your case is a one-shot job and you don't want to buy a bending iron, the poplar can be bent cold over a gentle radius—say, 12 in. If the ⅛-in. thickness doesn't seem strong enough, use two layers with glue in between.

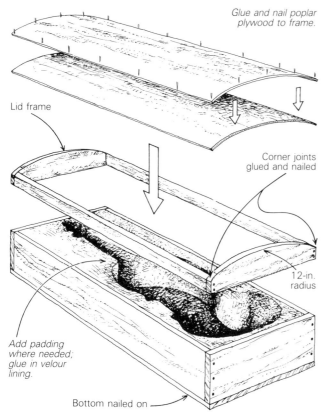

Glue and nail poplar plywood to frame.

Lid frame

Corner joints glued and nailed

12-in. radius

Add padding where needed; glue in velour lining.

Bottom nailed on

I suggest that you make the top frame and box out of poplar as well, as shown in the drawing above. Cases can be built quick and dirty, with glued and nailed butt joints. Attach the top to its frame with nails, screws or staples, to be covered later by the leatherette, which you can buy at local fabric or upholstery stores. A block of foam rubber cut out to match the violin's shape, with ½-in. clearance on all sides, will pad the instrument. Or you can cut the shape into a block of wood and then pad it with foam or cotton batting. Either way, line the padding with velour, yellow-glued in place. Bending poplar can be ordered from Allied Plywood, 1635 Poplar St., New York, N.Y. 10461.

Bending mandolin sides—*Currently I am making F-style mandolins, and am having a small problem with some of them. The sides, made of highly figured maple, are steam-*

bent. Occasionally I find splits on the surface of the wood after it has dried. These are not deep enough to present a structural problem, but they are too deep to be sanded out. Is there any type of glue that would fill these cracks, and still not repel a water-base or alcohol-base stain? Since I have to reject these, I'd very much like to solve this problem. I hate to see such beautiful wood go to waste.
—*Glenn J. Behrle, Milford, Conn.*

RICHARD NEWMAN REPLIES: First, it makes sense to attack this problem at its source—the bending process—and try to prevent the splits before you begin. Here are some of the questions you need to consider before and while you are bending: Is your maple wood at the optimum moisture content for bending (12% to 20%)? Is the wood thin enough for the bend? Is the material backed by a bending strip? Are there any tiny defects on the surface prior to bending? (The smallest tear-out paves the way for a serious split.) Are you steaming the wood too long and thereby weakening the stock?

Assuming that the splits still occur after you have done your best to minimize them, there are several possibilities for dealing with them. First, though, I don't know of any glue that will fill cracks and accept stain to match raw wood. Assuming you use a lacquer finish, you could stain the wood first, seal it, and then fill the cracks carefully. You might use a lacquer stick matched to the stained wood, or substitute a mixture of epoxy resin and stained wood dust. Alternatively, you could fill the cracks first and then use the color in your lacquer, instead of stain. This is done commercially and hides all sorts of problems, although it does obscure the figure of the wood.

My real feeling is that if you are making really fine and expensive instruments, you should continue to reject those that have imperfect sides. This is one good reason to consider making an inexpensive companion line of instruments that will allow you to use attractive but less than perfect materials, rather than waste them.

BILL CUMPIANO REPLIES: In response to Glenn Behrle's question on bending mandolin sides, I'd add that slats will crack at the curl interfaces if you, first, try to bend pieces of wood that are excessively thick and second, if you overwet and overheat them with steam. It's best to thin your slats to between ¹⁄₆₄ and ³⁄₃₂ in. and use a hot-pipe bending system, with a small-diameter (1½ in. to 2 in.) bending iron. Small slats will bend easily over a hot pipe after they have been dipped momentarily in water. No soaking or steaming is necessary. Be sure to adjust the pipe temperature to about 250°F, not so hot as to cause instant scorching when the piece is slowly worked over it.

Maple in thin strips bends very easily. So easily, in fact, that lute makers take their ¹⁄₁₆-in. curly slats and bend them dry over a hot pipe, or alternatively train a teakettle spout on the slats for 30 seconds and bend them with their fingers, using no pipe or form at all.

If you use slats that are more than ⅛ in. thick, you will get cracking along the curl when you use any of the above procedures, especially if you further soften the material with excessive steaming. Finally, for best results, select pieces that have tight, tiny curls rather than large, wavy ones. Not only do such pieces hold together far better, but they also yield a finer bent surface.

Preventing warp—*I was assembling a dulcimer for a friend of mine, and since she was in no hurry for it, I put it aside for some time while I worked on other pieces. Initially, I glued three braces across the grain on the ⅛-in.*

Q & A

cherry back. This was done at the first of the summer. By January, when I got around to working on the thing again, the back was conspicuously warped across the grain. I understand why it warped, but I'd like to know if there's any way I can prevent such warpage in the future. —Charles Kish, Saratoga Springs, N.Y.

THOMAS KNATT REPLIES: As you suspect, the ⅛-in. cherry shrank across the grain as it dried out in winter, but the braces could not shrink along their length. Thus, the cherry back warped. I live near Boston, and in our climate I do not glue on bracing, nor do I assemble tops and backs onto sides of guitars, between June 1 and October 1. I prefer to glue on bracing in the dead of winter, when everything is the driest. I put tops and backs onto sides in April and May. Then these have started to warp to a convex curve, and a little more wood is actually in the instrument between the bound edges. It can therefore straighten out more before it cracks or warps to a concave curve.

Also, the bracing on most guitars is convex; it is arched by sanding or by using a compass plane. Since the widest part of a dulcimer is usually about 6 in. to 8 in. across, if you arch the brace quite a bit (say, from 4mm to 5mm, from center to edge), that would probably be enough to keep the wood from going the other way.

Banjo-making—*I would like to make a banjo using materials and techniques from the 1880s. Can you recommend a book or other source of information? Under normal circumstances it would be easy for me to run down this information, but I am home-ported in Japan and am presently in the Arabian Sea.* —Lt. Robert E. Riess, USS White Plains

RICHARD NEWMAN REPLIES: Actually, banjo-making has not changed very much since the 1880s; in fact, I suspect some of my machinery dates from that period. Then, as now, there were classy makers in large cities catering to a very sophisticated market (the instrument was the rage for both classical and popular music at the time), while at the same time craftsmen in the Appalachian mountains were making simple, folksy instruments.

Materials have changed little: Hide glue has given way to more modern adhesives, lacquer has replaced French polish and varnish, but it seems that the quality of ebony and mahogany has deteriorated. The techniques of that time no doubt varied with the skill and ingenuity of the maker, just as they do today. Suffice it to say that most of the work was done by hand, probably with fewer and simpler tools than most of us now possess.

As to design, again rather little has changed. The rim would be thin, perhaps ¼ in. or ⅜ in., with a thin (0.025 in. to 0.050 in.) covering of nickel-silver spun on after lamination. The entire instrument would be more delicate; banjos back then used gut strings, which caused less stress on the instrument than the steel strings of the present day. Of course there would be no resonator.

Very little information is available in print on banjo-making. Building an Appalachian banjo is covered in *Foxfire 3* (Doubleday, 245 Park Ave., New York, N.Y. 10167). There is also a chapter on building in the book *Earl Scruggs and the Five String Banjo* (Peer International Corp., 1619 Broadway, New York, N.Y. 10019). I also recommend the *Banjo Newsletter* (Box 364, Greensboro, Md. 21639), a monthly devoted to the five-string banjo. It has a column on construction, although it is modern rather than historical.

The best way to learn is to get a fine old banjo and try to copy it. A little advice from an experienced woodworker and hands-on experience are the best teachers.

Aztec Drum

Resonating tongues produce sound

by Ray Nitta

The drum is probably the earliest and most universal musical instrument. Used in initiation rites, magic, dance, religious ceremony, war, rock concert or symphonic orchestra, the hypnotic effect of rhythmic drumming is known to all cultures and peoples.

The instrument described here is patterned after the teponaztli, an ancient Aztec drum. Unlike the conventional skin-covered membranophone, the teponaztli was a unique idiophonic instrument with tongue-like protrusions to produce the sound. Perhaps best described as a two-keyed xylophone, the teponaztli resembled a narrow wooden barrel laid sideways. An H-shaped incision cut laterally into the top formed two tongues that vibrated when struck. The teponaztli was tuned by altering the thicknesses of these tongues to create different pitches, the most desirable being those with intervals a minor or major third apart. The hollow interior of the drum was its resonant chamber and a rectangular opening on the bottom of the instrument increased its volume, like the acoustical port on a guitar. The teponaztli was placed on a stand and played with rubber-tipped mallets (cured latex).

I have used the sound-producing principles of the teponaztli to make the drums shown here. The design, tongue proportions and resonant chamber have been carefully worked out to produce a pleasant progression of natural tones with good volume ranging around minor and major thirds to diminished and perfect fifths, just as in the original drum. The two tongues used by the Aztecs have been increased to six: three low-pitched bass tones and three contrasting higher ones. The woods used by the Aztecs can be expanded to include other resonant hard and soft woods such as padauk, redwood, bubinga, fir and Hawaiian koa.

Multiple factors govern the sound produced by this drum, among them the size and shape of the resonant cavity, the length and width of the tongues and the environment in which the drum is played. Any wood may be used for the sides and bottom of the drum, but the type (hard or soft) and grain of the top govern the sound. A softwood top makes a low thud. I advise using an even-grained hardwood: The harder the wood, the more crisp and metallic the sound.

The dimensions and proportions used here are to give the woodworker a concrete example to follow. However, there are no limits to what can be done to modify this basic design or to create a new one.

Cut the wood to the dimensions shown. The top slab is where the sound-producing tongues are to be cut. The 1/8-in. lauan ply on the bottom acts as a pliant membrane that mellows the tones. Remember to allow enough wood for the corner joinery. Although simple butt joints work well,

From *Fine Woodworking* magazine (Fall 1977) 8:72-73

Six-tongued drums of various woods. Inlaid dots mark location of purest tones. Drumsticks are 3/8-in. dowels fitted with superballs.

A dovetailed drum ready to assemble and cut. Butt joints, locking miters or rabbets may also be used to join sides.

dovetails, locking miters or rabbets enhance the strength and beauty of the corners.

Make an acoustical port with about the area of a silver dollar in one of the long side pieces. This opening supports the bass tones and amplifies the sound. Carefully glue the pieces into a well-sealed box. I find that vibration-resistant aliphatic resin glue works best.

Draw the tongues onto the top as shown in the diagram. Drill eight 3/8-in. holes at the tongue bases to serve as slit stops. Cut the tongue pattern with a saber saw. If the resultant pitches don't ring clear, enlarge the base holes to 1/2 in. or even 5/8 in. This will narrow the base of the tongues and make them more flexible.

Gluing the box together before cutting the tongues, a reversal of usual procedure, allows the maker to experiment with tones. By starting the cutting in the center (without pre-drilling slit stops), the maker can cut, strike the drum, cut again, and so on until the desired tone is achieved. The top is firmly supported on all edges and is unlikely to split.

Now tap along the length of each tongue with a drumstick and mark the spots where the pitch seems purest, with the

fewest overtones. These nodes are the spots to aim for when playing the drum. While they can be marked with paint, inlaid wood is prettier. I drill with a 1/2-in. spade or Forstner bit and plug with a 1/2-in. dowel, then sand smooth.

To finish the drum, round and form the edges with a drawknife and a plane. Sand with 80-grit garnet, then 120, and finish with 220. I use three coats of Watco and apply the final coat with 600 wet or dry sandpaper.

Make the drumsticks from 3/8-in. dowels 12 in. long, and 10-cent superballs from a toy store. Drill the balls with an 11/16-in. bit and press on.

Stands should be made to keep the drum from rattling when played on the floor or table and to increase its resonance. Good cushioning pads can be made from 1/2-in. foam or felt glued to matching blocks of wood.

The drum is magic. Place it on the foam stands, cradle it in your arm or set it on your lap. Start by playing softly; try to sustain a simple beat (about heartbeat tempo). Become one with the sound, let it move and merge with the natural rhythms of your body, feel its influence and power to move you physically, emotionally and spiritually.　　□

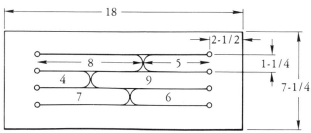

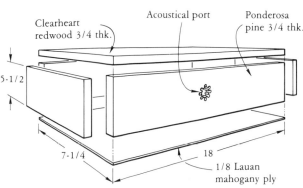

Author and drum. Nitta teaches curriculum development to teachers in Berkeley, Calif. His Aztec drum was designed as a project for beginners in school shops on restricted budgets.

Left, these tongue lengths produce pleasing bass and treble tones. Woods and dimensions can be changed to suit the maker.

it across the underside of the soundboard. This cross-grain brace helps resist the downward pressure of the bridge and reduces the chance of the soundboard splitting.

Now you're ready to glue the soundboard to the rim. Hold the banjo in a machine vise by the part of the neck that passes through the rim. Spread glue on the upper edge of the rim and set the soundboard in place. Be sure that the flat section of the disc is lined up where the neck joins the rim and that the soundboard overhangs the rim evenly all around.

For a good glue job, it's important to apply gentle clamping pressure at every point on the rim. When the glue is dry, use the bandsaw to trim the soundboard flush with the rim.

Fingerboard—A fingerboard that contrasts in color with the neck of the banjo is appealing. Mountain folk used native woods: walnut, cherry or maple would work well. No part of the instrument receives more wear and tear, so very dense woods are best—the finest banjos have ebony or rosewood fingerboards.

Cut a piece of stock slightly wider than the neck and a couple of inches longer than its length. Joint one face and one edge, then thickness the piece to about ¼ in. Pencil a line up the center of the stock and lay out the shape of the fingerboard centered on this line. If you want frets, mark the position of each fret along the jointed edge of the stock, then use a square to project each mark across the fingerboard.

Fretwire has a T-shaped cross section and the shank of the T is jammed into a slot in the fingerboard. You'll need about 5 ft. of fretwire and a fretsaw, or a dovetail saw whose kerf gives a snug fit to your particular fretwire. If the saw cuts too wide, you can narrow the kerf by sliding a file lightly along the sides of the saw, reducing the set of the saw's teeth. Don't make the kerf too tight or the neck will bow when you hammer all the frets in. Guide the saw against a block of wood clamped to the fingerboard, as shown in the photo below. This block can also serve as a depth stop. Trim its height so that the back of the dovetail saw catches on its top edge when the cut is to depth—about ⅟₁₆ in. deeper than the shank of the fret. Practice cutting frets in scrap before trying it on your fingerboard.

After you've cut all the fret slots, saw the fingerboard to shape and glue it to the neck. Be sure that the centerline of the fingerboard is true to the centerline of the neck and that the end butts up against the flat section of the soundboard. Use a scrap of

To saw the fretwire slot, guide the saw against a block of wood clamped to the fingerboard. Trim the block height so that the back of the dovetail saw catches on its top edge when the cut is about ⅟₁₆ in. deeper than the shank of the fretwire.

wood roughly the size of the fingerboard as a caul to distribute the clamping pressure. Now bandsaw the sides of the neck to match the shape of the fingerboard.

Carving the neck—Carving the back of the neck is probably the fussiest job in this project. The curve in cross section must be rounded almost to the top edge of the fingerboard, while the shape along the length is almost a straight line. At the same time, the neck gets slightly wider and thicker from the nut to the rim and is faired gently into the peg head and heel. Rough out the shape with a spokeshave and refine it with a scraper or file. Sandpaper on a hard block works best for truing the surface lengthwise. A well-shaped neck is a musician's joy, so examine your work with your fingers, as well as your eyes. It's helpful to handle a completed banjo to get an idea of how a neck should feel.

Fretting—Inject a small amount of white or yellow glue in the fret's kerf and tap in a length of fretwire using a lightweight, deadblow hammer. Be sure to support the neck with a block of wood directly under the fret you're installing. Using a pair of nipping pliers, trim the overhanging ends of the fretwire. File the ends even with the fingerboard and round them slightly at the top, so no sharp edges protrude. If you file the wrong way, you'll lift the fretwire. To remove the file burrs, sand the edges of the fingerboard with 220-grit paper on a hard block. Run a long file lengthwise up and down the neck to level any high frets.

Now you can smooth the outer edge of the rim with a spokeshave and sandpaper, and finish-sand the whole instrument.

Set-up—Install tuning pegs according to the manufacturer's instructions, or make your own tapered friction pegs. To guide the fifth string over the fifth fret, we cut a simple notch in the fingerboard. You could also insert a small round-head wood screw between the fourth and fifth frets so that the head of the screw holds the string down tight on the fifth fret. Instead of a tailpiece, we used five round-head brass brads driven into undersized holes at the tail end of the instrument. These brads secure the ends of the strings. Be sure that the heads of the brads stand about ⅟₃₂ in. proud to catch the string's loop. Round the edge of the soundboard slightly where the strings bear on the corner. Fashion a nut and bridge from dense hardwood, and trim their height to give the proper action (the height of the strings at the nut and last fret). The nut glues against the peg head and the end of the fingerboard. File shallow notches for each string. String the banjo and position the bridge so that the 12th fret is midway between the nut and bridge. Adjust the bridge so that holding down each string at the 12th fret produces a tone one octave higher than the open string. Move the bridge slightly closer to the nut if the octave is flat, further away if it is sharp. Don't glue the bridge to the soundboard. The tension of the strings will hold it in place.

An oil finish, wet-sanded with 400-grit wet-or-dry paper, will give you a fine-looking and serviceable musical instrument. A good book for beginners is *How to Play the 5-String Banjo* by Pete Seeger (Oak Publications, Div. of Music Sales Corp., 799 Broadway, New York, N.Y. 10003). Good playing! □

Richard Starr teaches woodworking at Richmond Middle School in Hanover, N.H., and is the author of the book Woodworking with Kids *(The Taunton Press, 1982). Photos by the author. Banjo tuning pegs and strings are available from Stewart-MacDonald Mfg. Co., Box 900, Athens, Ohio 45701.*

The Flageolet

Basic woodwind is turning, drilling exercise

by Kent Forrester

Over the last couple of centuries, most woodwind instruments (flutes, clarinets, oboes and others) have accumulated a bewildering variety of keys, levers, springs, bushings and extra note holes. Because of this, making a woodwind instrument seems beyond the skill of the average woodturner. However, stripped of modern embellishments, woodwinds make interesting and relatively easy woodturning projects.

The modest little woodwind known as the flageolet is not as versatile as a clarinet and not as pretentious as an oboe (you'll never get a job playing it in the Philharmonic). But it has nevertheless been a favorite of musicians for centuries—the 17th-century diarist, Samuel Pepys, loved his flageolet almost as much as he loved barmaids. With a pleasant, high-pitched piping sound and a range of more than two octaves, the flageolet can be used both for accompaniment (it goes particularly well with guitars and voice in folk music) and for solos.

To make a flageolet, first cut a 1-in. turning square 14 in. long out of the best hardwood you have. Cherry, walnut and maple are fine for flageolets; rosewood, cocobolo and ebony are even more handsome.

The boring operation will require support for the tailstock end of the wood. Buy a brass or steel plumbing tee with an inside diameter of at least 1/2 in. and an outside diameter of no more than 7/8 in. Also pick up a 4-1/2-in. long piece of pipe, threaded on one end, that can be screwed into the bottom of the tee. This pipe will be mounted in the lathe's tool post.

Now drill a hole about 3/8 in. deep in the center of the end of the stock, of the same diameter as the outside diameter of the tee. Drill a 1/2-in. starter hole for your bit in the center of the previous hole. Because the stock will be turning on the tee, rub soap inside the larger hole to reduce friction.

Now mount the stock between a headstock spur and the tee jig. With the tee loose in the tool post, pull it up so that the end of the tee enters the hole in the stock. Mount a 1/2-in. twist drill bit in a chuck in the tailstock and push this bit into the starter hole in the stock. This

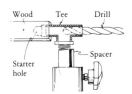

will center the tee on the lathe. Cinch up the tee tightly, lock it to the tool post and lock the tool post to the lathe bed.

A 1/2-in. shell auger mounted in the tailstock will bore a straight, smooth hole. A bell hanger's bit (of the type electricians use) or a 1/2-in. twist drill mounted on a bit extender

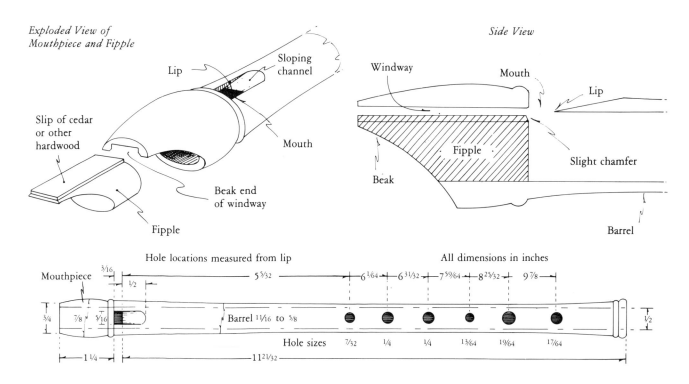

Exploded View of Mouthpiece and Fipple

Lip

Sloping channel

Slip of cedar or other hardwood

Mouth

Beak end of windway

Fipple

Side View

Windway

Mouth

Lip

Beak

Fipple

Slight chamfer

Barrel

Hole locations measured from lip

All dimensions in inches

Mouthpiece

3/16

1/2

5 5/32

6 1/64 — 6 31/32 — 7 59/64 — 8 25/32 — 9 7/8

3/4

7/8

5/16

Barrel 11/16 to 5/8

1/2

Hole sizes   7/32   1/4   1/4   13/64   19/64   17/64

1 1/4

11 21/32

The flageolet is basically a whistle; sound is produced when wind hits sharpened edge of lip, formed by filing sloping channel in front of mouth, left. Note hole locations are carefully measured from lip, right.

Flageolet is held in V-block, left, to file channel behind mouth that forms upper surface of windway. To sand inside of bore, right, garnet paper is wrapped and glued around dowel and chucked in lathe.

will also do the job. These bits will drift a little, but the stock is cut oversize to allow for it.

Carefully measure the distance to the spur and stick a piece of masking tape on the bit where it must stop. Run the lathe at its slowest speed, drill slowly and clear the chips frequently. Now remove the stock from the lathe and saw off the end, in small increments, until the hole appears.

To facilitate turning, plane or saw off the corners from the 1-in. stock. Now place a cone-shaped abrasive wheel with a 1/4-in. or 1/2-in. shank in a chuck in the headstock and a cone center in the tailstock. Mount the wood between these two cones and cinch up tightly so that the abrasive cone grabs the stock and turns it. Turn the flageolet to shape and sand.

Begin shaping the mouth by drilling two or three 5/32-in. diameter holes. Then file to the dimensions of the rectangular shape, as shown in the drawing. Now measure from the lip and drill the six note holes. To sand the inside of the bore, wrap and glue sandpaper around a 3/8-in. dowel and chuck the dowel in the lathe. Then turn on the lathe and run the bore over the sandpaper until it is smooth. Smoothness is important, so go down to 120 or 220 grit.

To make the windway, use a flat file that is 5/16 in. wide or less. File a channel at the center of the top of the bore until the underside edge of the area that will form the lip is flat. Cut and file the sloping channel that forms the sharp edge of the lip. Now finish filing the channel back of the mouth, to form the upper surface of the windway. A piece of soft wood or leather in the mouth will prevent the file from damaging the lip. Continue filing until the lip, as you sight down the windway, is about 1/64 in. below the top of the windway.

To make the fipple, cut a 1/2-in hardwood dowel to length and sand a flat that is 5/16 in. wide. On this flat, glue (with waterproof glue) a slip about 1/16 in. thick of maple, cherry or cedar. If you use maple or cherry, coat the surface with var-

nish to prevent the grain from rising. Moisture has so little effect on cedar that all it needs is a coat of penetrating oil. Sand this slip until it is 1/64 in. below the lip when, fipple in place, you sight down the windway. The height of the windway at the mouth end will now be 1/32 in. and the lip will appear in the center of the windway. The height of the windway at the beak end is not critical, but 1/16 in. or a little more is about right. Now cut the beak to shape.

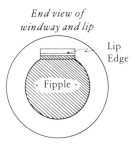

End view of windway and lip

Lip Edge

Fipple

To hold the flageolet, let the instrument rest on your thumbs and use the first three fingers of each hand to cover the six note holes. Rest the mouthpiece between your lips and blow with sufficient strength to produce a soft, steady tone.

The primary scale is produced by uncovering each hole in order. The lowest note, "C," is produced when all holes are covered. The semi-tones (half-notes) are produced by withdrawing the tip of your fingers so that they cover only half the holes. The second octave is achieved by blowing harder.

Test your flageolet by running through at least two octaves. If the low notes are very weak (almost inaudible), remove the fipple and increase the chamfer or sand the fipple lower. If the high notes will not blow, you have sanded the fipple too low.

Coat the fipple with hot wax before insertion, to eliminate air leaks between it and the bore. Finish bore and exterior with a few coats of penetrating oil or varnish. □

Kent Forrester, associate professor of English at Murray State University, Murray, Ky., researches and builds medieval, Renaissance, and 18th-century woodwind instruments.

World Globe
Jig cuts segments for hollow sphere

by Steven A. Hartley

I had been thinking about making a wooden world globe long before I seriously planned the project. I pondered its size, the kind of wood and the surface treatment I would be able to give it, and as I did so my enthusiasm grew. But putting the idea into action presented the problem of making a sphere from which to make the globe. A fair amount of research revealed nothing about wooden spheres, let alone world globes of wood. Thus the method offered here is the result of my own trials and errors.

My globe is a hollow sphere made of 76 identical segments, each of them a quarter-circle in section, cut from 1½-in. thick sugar pine. I made the sphere in two halves, rabbetted together at the equator. It is 18 in. in diameter and the wall is a uniform ¾ in. thick. First I bandsawed the segments to their quarter-circle profile. Then I used the table saw and a jig I devised to make them wedge-shaped.

Make the segment layout template out of ¼-in. Masonite, as shown. Its width represents the thickness of the finished globe. Use the template to lay out stock for 76 segments plus a few extra, paying attention to the grain direction of the stock. You want a strong globe, so you must leave the long fibers of the wood relatively intact. The pieces may be cut freehand on the band saw, but stay close to the line, especially on the outside radius. This will save handwork later on.

Cutting the segments   After the segments have been bandsawn, make the segment slicing jig. The drawing is dimensioned to fit my Rockwell saw—you may have to revise it

Photos: Steven and Tina Hartley

Hollow globe has carved ocean currents, smooth continents.

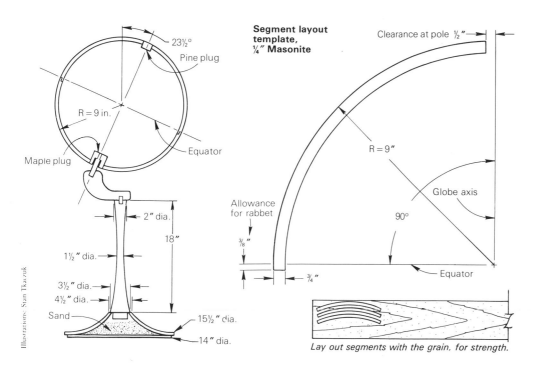

Segment layout template, ¼″ Masonite

Clearance at pole ½″

R = 9″

Globe axis

90°

Allowance for rabbet

⅜″

¾″

Equator

Lay out segments with the grain. for strength.

23½°

Pine plug

R = 9 in.

Maple plug

Equator

2″ dia.

18″

1½″ dia.

3½″ dia.

4½″ dia.

Sand

15½″ dia.

14″ dia.

Illustrations: Stan Tkaczuk

Bandsaw 76 blanks.

From *Fine Woodworking* magazine (January 1979) 14:61-65

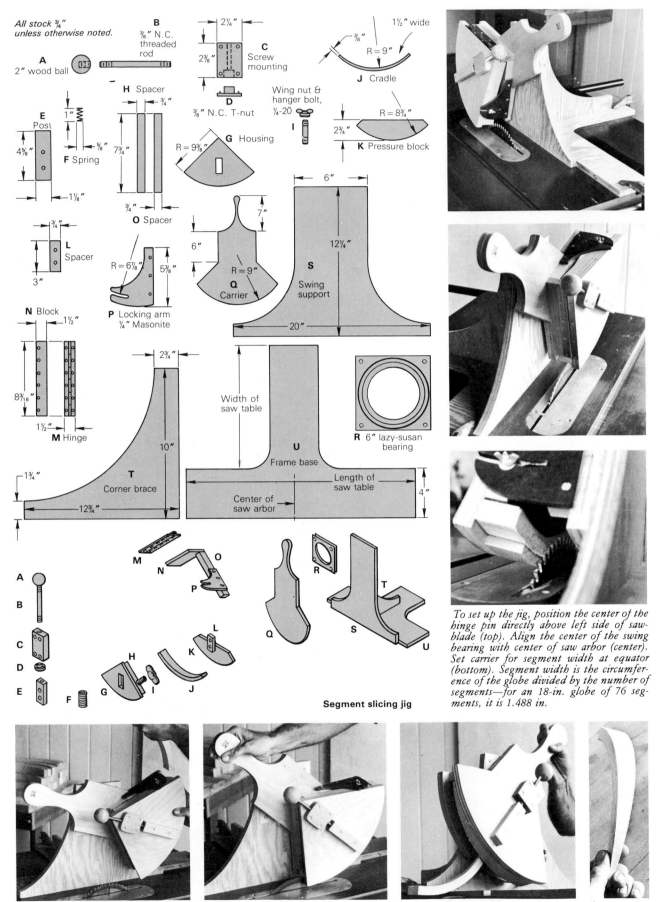

All stock ¾"
unless otherwise noted.

A 2" wood ball

B ⅜" N.C. threaded rod

C Screw mounting 2¼" 2⅛"

D ⅜" N.C. T-nut

E Post 4⅝" 1⅛"

F Spring 1" ⅝"

H Spacer 7¾" ¾" ¾"

I Wing nut & hanger bolt, ¼-20

G Housing R = 9⅜"

J Cradle 1½" wide ⅜" R = 9"

K Pressure block R = 8¾" 2¾"

O Spacer

L Spacer ¾" 3"

P Locking arm ¼" Masonite R = 6⅞" 5⅜"

Q Carrier 6" 7" R = 9" 6"

S Swing support 6" 12¼" 20"

N Block 1½" 8³⁄₁₆" 1½"

M Hinge

R 6" lazy-susan bearing

T Corner brace 2¾" 10" 1¾" 12¾"

U Frame base Width of saw table Length of saw table Center of saw arbor 4"

A B C D E F G H I J K L M N O P Q R S T U

Segment slicing jig

To set up the jig, position the center of the hinge pin directly above left side of sawblade (top). Align the center of the swing bearing with center of saw arbor (center). Set carrier for segment width at equator (bottom). Segment width is the circumference of the globe divided by the number of segments—for an 18-in. globe of 76 segments, it is 1.488 in.

To use the jig, insert blank and tighten wooden knob. Swing the jig through the sawblade. The scrap falls clear, leaving a sphere segment.

to suit your own saw. All materials in the jig must be perfectly flat to ensure smooth operation. A 6-in. lazy-Susan bearing attaches the carrier to the frame. Check the bearing for play between its two plates. If it is loose, you'll have to crimp the inner lip with pliers.

The cradle portion of the clamping mechanism, which is only ⅜ in. thick, should be made of maple or birch, because it is subjected to constant pressure in use. This part (J) will be cut to final shape while the jig slices the first segment.

The hinge that attaches the clamp section to the carrier represents the axis of the sphere. The distance between the clamp section and the sawblade at the rear end of the cradle represents the widest point of each segment at the equator. This is determined by dividing the number of segments into the circumference of the sphere. In the case of my 18-in. globe this dimension is 1.488 in., or about 1³¹⁄₆₄ in. This measurement is most critical and should be checked periodically while cutting the segments.

The segment clamping device applies uniform pressure to the segment and holds it firmly while cutting. You may think that the tightening screw should be placed over the pressure block for more direct pressure. I tried this and found it difficult to operate because it was too close to the swing handle. Placement as shown holds fine and is easier to operate. Remember, you have to loosen and tighten the screw 152 times to make a sphere.

Oil the bearing and wax all moving parts before assembly. They should be close-fitting yet move freely. Clamp the jig to the saw table so that the center of swing is over the center of the saw arbor. The carrier must be parallel to the sawblade,

and the blade must be square with the table. Elevate the blade ⅛ in. above the mounted segment.

To use the jig, swing it up above the front of the blade and hold it there by grasping the clamp section. Now slide a segment in from the front. Clamp it in place with the edge closest to you flush with the edge of the jig. Your hand on the tightening screw will hold the jig in position while you reach for the swing handle. Turn on the power and carefully swing the segment through the saw in one continuous motion. The scrap will fall clear of the blade when the cut is completed. Then swing the segment back through the saw to its starting position for the next cut. Be sure to hold the sawn segment while loosening the clamp, lest it slide through into the blade. Repeat this process, cutting all 76 segments. Save the scrap—it will be used to make the base for the globe.

Assembling the sphere   When all the segments are cut, make an assembly fixture from three pieces of plywood. Cut a circular hole 18 in. in diameter out of one of the pieces of plywood, and secure it on top of the base piece. The third gets a hole around 14 in. in diameter. This piece will be used to apply clamping pressure.

Set up a hemisphere in the assembly fixture. The accuracy necessary to have all of these pieces fall together perfectly is beyond the capabilities of the segment jig and the table saw, so some variation is almost certain to occur. If you're within ⅛ in. oversize or undersize at the equator, you are as close as you could expect—within .0065 in. per segment.

If you are slightly oversize, trim several segments, using the jig. Do not try to alter one segment to accommodate the

The segments spiral around the pole. Adjust several segments to make them all fit, then glue and clamp with aid of plywood jig.

Whittle a plug to fill the hole, then bore a clean 2-in. hole at each pole to receive turned plugs. The hemispheres are shaped with a compass plane and Surform, then a rabbet is routed at the equator.

Small Projects

EDITOR'S NOTE: Small projects have a special appeal—they might be finished in a weekend. There is always someone, including yourself, who deserves some of your shop time, even if there's very little time to spare. The ideas that follow below and on the next three pages require various levels of woodworking skills. They were selected from *Fine Woodworking* magazine's file of reader-contributed, simple and elegant small projects.

Candelabra from Chinese ideograms

by Warren Durbin

I have always admired the line quality of Chinese calligraphy and wanted to express its elegance and serenity in a usable object. Last winter I started work on a series of candelabra; the ones pictured here draw their inspiration from Chinese characters relating to shelter. I was interested in the interplay between light and shadow and so contrasted Gabon ebony with maple, and teak with oak. The small scale of the project makes it possible to use precious but otherwise wasted scraps.

The candelabra shown below are about 15 in. by 6½ in. by 2½ in. But really the only dimensional constraints involve the candles themselves, which are a standard ⅞-in. diameter at the base. The rest of the shape is an aesthetic matter, and variations are possible. Bandsawing the top and bottom pieces, first in profile then in plan, reveals both radial and tangential grain patterns. I use a spokeshave, scrapers and sandpaper to take these to their final shapes, concentrating on symmetrical and fair curves. I make the uprights next, mortising in squared stock for the one or two horizontal cross pieces. Once again with spokeshave and scrapers, I take the uprights to final shape. To maintain their original integrity, I use bridle joints in the ends to connect the pieces. I make the delicate cuts along the grain with a Japanese backsaw (*dozuki*), then chisel carefully across the grain to remove the waste. The horizontal yoke piece or pieces, made next, fit the mortises in the uprights and accentuate the curves of the top and bottom pieces.

At this stage, with the stand dry-assembled, I mark the candle sockets for drilling, then disassemble to drill, though drilling could be done when the top piece is squared stock. For final assembly, I do not glue the yokes, only the bridle joints, clamping them lightly.

Oriental characters can provide inspiration for objects and furniture of various scales, including tables and chairs. It is a matter of abstracting the shapes of the original brush strokes and applying them to a functional structure. The success of the piece, as in calligraphy itself, depends on the balance and interplay of the separate lines and surfaces.

Warren Durbin makes furniture and wooden accessories in his shop in Burlington, Vt.

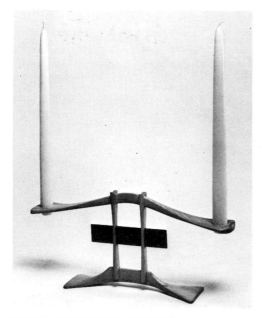

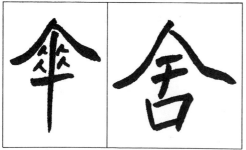

Candelabrum of teak and oak, right, inspired by the Chinese character for home, above right. Candelabrum of maple and ebony, top, inspired by the character for umbrella, above left.

From *Fine Woodworking* magazine (November 1980) 25:60-63

Bob Barrett

Horses and wagon

by Robert Ruffner

A simple piece with old-fashioned charm, this horse-and-wagon toy is made of poplar, walnut and birch. Variations are easy enough. The basic procedures are given in the drawing below.

Robert Ruffner lives in Irvine, Ky.

Carolyn Whitesal

Plan for horses and wagon

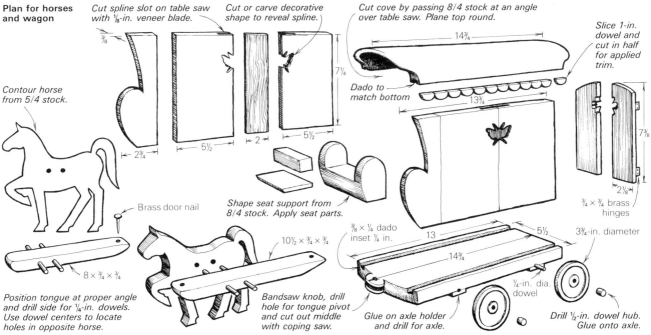

Cut spline slot on table saw with ⅛-in. veneer blade.

Cut or carve decorative shape to reveal spline.

Cut cove by passing 8/4 stock at an angle over table saw. Plane top round.

Slice 1-in. dowel and cut in half for applied trim.

Contour horse from 5/4 stock.

Dado to match bottom

¾ × ¾ brass hinges

Brass door nail

Shape seat support from 8/4 stock. Apply seat parts.

Position tongue at proper angle and drill side for ¼-in. dowels. Use dowel centers to locate holes in opposite horse.

Bandsaw knob, drill hole for tongue pivot and cut out middle with coping saw.

⅜ × ¼ dado inset ¼ in.

Glue on axle holder and drill for axle.

¼-in. dia. dowel

3¾-in. diameter

Drill ½-in. dowel hub. Glue onto axle.

8 × ¾ × ¾

10½ × ¾ × ¾

A triangular drop-leaf table with rotating top

by Pendleton Tompkins

The advantage of a triangular table is that the sitters can face inward. The area of this tabletop becomes a circle when the leaves are raised and the top rotated 60°; the corners of the base then support the leaves. Any hardwood will do.

Make the legs first; they are flat-faced where they meet the aprons but taper to the foot with a graduated curve on the inside and fall straight along a 60° corner on the outside. To shape the legs I built a jig, basically a long, narrow frame in which the leg blank is held and rotated between two centers as it is passed over the jointer. The same operation can be performed with a router and jig, though the most straightforward way to cut the taper and graduated curve is with a sharp block plane and a spokeshave. Detail *A* (on the next page) shows the sections of curve and taper. With the legs shaped, cut the mortises for the apron tenons—no deeper than ⅝ in. or you will weaken the legs.

Before cutting the aprons to length,

Foto Associates West

The drop-leaves of this clever sidetable are supported by the base itself when the top is rotated 120°. It's a good project for practicing the rule joint, the mortise and tenon and the shaping of tapered legs.

Things to Make **69**

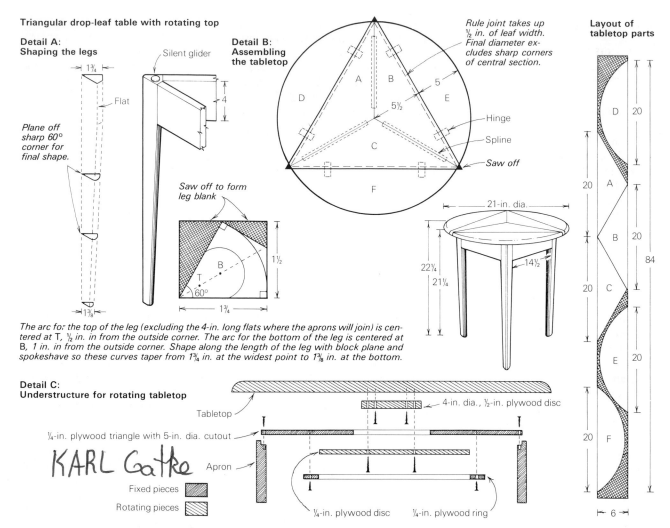

Triangular drop-leaf table with rotating top

Detail A:
Shaping the legs

Silent glider

1¾

Flat

Plane off
sharp 60°
corner for
final shape.

Saw off to form
leg blank

4

B

T
60°

1½

1¾

1⅜

Detail B:
**Assembling
the tabletop**

Rule joint takes up
½ in. of leaf width.
Final diameter ex-
cludes sharp corners
of central section.

**Layout of
tabletop parts**

D

A

B

E

5

5½

C

F

Hinge

Spline

Saw off

21-in. dia.

22¼
21¼

14½

D 20

20 A 20

B 20 84

C 20

E 20

F 20

6

The arc for the top of the leg (excluding the 4-in. long flats where the aprons will join) is centered at T, ½ in. in from the outside corner. The arc for the bottom of the leg is centered at
B, 1 in. in from the outside corner. Shape along the length of the leg with block plane and
spokeshave so these curves taper from 1¾ in. at the widest point to 1⅜ in. at the bottom.

Detail C:
Understructure for rotating tabletop

Tabletop

4-in. dia., ½-in. plywood disc

¼-in. plywood triangle with 5-in. dia. cutout

KARL Gatke

Apron

Fixed pieces

Rotating pieces

¼-in. plywood disc   ¼-in. plywood ring

spline together the three triangles that form the center of the top; cut the rule joints (which hide the knuckle hinges) between this section and the three drop-leaves. All six pieces can be laid out and sawn from a 7-ft. long 1x6, as shown in detail B. With the hinges mounted, first bandsaw the top roughly round, then trim it to a circle with a router mounted on a plywood trammel that pivots on a temporary screw block in the center of the tabletop bottom. Note that the 5½-in. wide leaves have lost ½ in. to the rule joint and that the final diameter of the tabletop (21 in.) excludes the sharp corners of the central section. The edge can be molded to taste.

Now cut a tenon on one end of each of the three aprons and fit two aprons into one leg. Lay the hinged tabletop upside-down on the workbench, turn up two leaves and fit the leg with aprons into the angle between the leaves. Cut the aprons to a length that, with the re-maining two legs attached, will exactly fit the tabletop with the leaves folded. Cut tenons and fit the legs and remain-

ing apron together. Before assembling, cut a ¼-in. rabbet on the top inside edge of the aprons to receive a plywood triangle, yet to be made. Gluing up the legs and aprons requires a deft touch; it's best to fit the tenons a bit at a time in sequence and use a strap clamp to bring the joints together.

While the glue is drying, cut a tri-angle from ¼-in. plywood to fit in the apron rabbets. Then cut a 5-in. dia-meter hole in the center of the plywood, and screw and glue the plywood into the rabbeted aprons.

Now cut a ¼-in. plywood disc just large enough to fit snugly inside the tri-angle formed by the legs and aprons. Cut from within this disc another disc of 1-in. shorter radius, producing also a 1-in. wide ring with an entrance kerf that can later adjust the ring's size. Both discs should be near-perfect circles; the inner one must turn smoothly within the outer ring, so use an accurate circle-cutting jig to make this cut. Sand the saw kerf lightly. Center the outer ring inside the aprons and glue and screw it

to the underside of the plywood triangle in the table. To ease the top's move-ment over the base, drive ⅝-in. silent gliders into the top of each leg.

Once again with the hinged tabletop upside-down on the bench, set the base inside the triangular center section. From ½-in. plywood cut a 4-in. diam-eter disc and screw it to the underside of the tabletop approximately in the center, inside the 5-in. diameter hole that you've already cut in the plywood triangle. Take care not to screw into the splined joints of the top. Now place the disc of ¼-in. plywood within the outer ring and screw it to the disc of ½-in. plywood; detail C shows the relation of these parts. When the table is lifted by its top, this set of screws will hold the base on, so use screws long enough to enter the top. But before driving more than a couple, rotate the base 120° in each direction to see if the leaves can be folded without interference.

*Pendleton Tompkins, a surgeon, lives in
San Mateo, Calif.*

Flip-open box from one piece of wood

by Daniel Mosheim

I've been making these boxes as gifts for a couple of years, and each one has proved popular and challenging to make. The design can be adapted to many uses with only slight changes. Here I'll cover the most complex one I've done, for business cards. I've fed the woodstove with one or two of these; you can spoil it with the last pass of the plane so work carefully and don't rush.

I've used apple, maple, chestnut, walnut and cherry, but quartersawn zebrawood remains my favorite. In general the darker and more straight-grained the hardwood, the better the overall effect. To start, you will need a piece about 3¼ in. by 6 in. by ¾ in., with faces and edges straight and parallel. Strike a witness mark across the face, as shown in figure 1. Put a sharp blade in your table saw and check your fence settings on scrap wood before making each cut on your good stock. You have four ripping cuts to make; after planing and scraping the edges smooth and pressing them together to check the fit, you should have two pieces about 5/16 in. wide, two pieces 1/16 in. wide and one piece that is slightly wider than your business card, usually 2 in. Place your card on the face of this piece and mark the center and a little past the ends of the card. Lightly square these marks around the pieces and make a ¼-in. slot for half the card all the way through the width of the stock, as shown in figure 2. I use a ¼-in. bit in the drill press to rough it out and a sharp chisel to true up the walls. Get this slot smooth now, it's your last chance.

Now glue the two 1/16-in. pieces to this center one, using your witness marks and all the clamps you have room for. Get good glue lines here. After the glue dries, cut a second slot through the width of the stock for the rest of the length of the card (figure 3). This slot will open into the first slot between the two 1/16-in. pieces. Don't spend a lot of time here because you can smooth this slot after the next two cuts. Using a beveled scrap block as a guide, cut with a backsaw two 45° angles at the ends of the second slot, *A* and *B* in figure 3. Separate the halves and smooth the insides. The ends of the slot at *C* and *D* can be cut on the table saw with the miter guide and your blade set at the right height. Be careful to keep your fingers where they belong.

Put all the pieces back together, including the two outside 5/16-in. pieces, and clamp them temporarily. To locate centers for the dowel hinges, strike a sharp line across the face of the pieces ¼ in. from the end of the first slot, at *E* in figure 4. Unclamp the three pieces and continue line *E* down the outside edges of the assembly and down the inside edges of the 5/16-in. pieces. With a marking gauge set to half the thickness of your stock, mark four points on these lines. Be accurate; the location of the dowel hinge is critical for your box to open and close properly. Using a 3/16-in. bit, drill into the center assembly to a depth of ⅜ in. and halfway through the thickness of the 5/16-in. pieces. Cut and place the dowels and put the whole thing back together again. If everything seems to fit and the box opens and closes, you're ready to glue. Paste-wax the sides of the big half of the center assembly and put a thin coat of glue on the sides of the small half and on the mating surface of each of the 5/16-in. pieces. Glue neatly so you have a minimum of cleaning up to do inside. And don't forget to put in the dowel hinges. Clamp lightly and open and close the box. If it works, clamp tightly.

When it's dry, cut the box to final length, shape it and finish it as you like. Be careful during the shaping that you don't cut away too much of the bevel or you'll have a gap to the inside and some fuel for the woodstove. □

Fig. 1: Ripping the stock

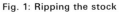

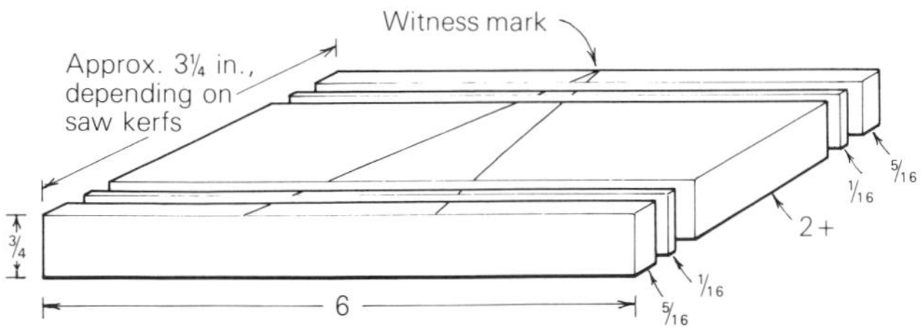
Witness mark
Approx. 3¼ in., depending on saw kerfs
5/16
1/16
2+
¾
6
1/16
5/16

Fig. 2: Cutting the first slot

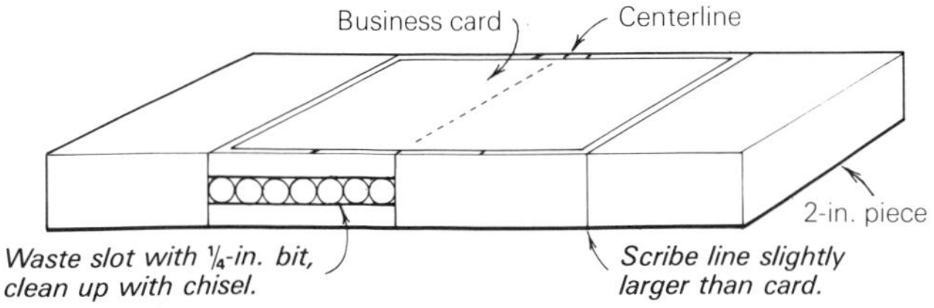
Business card
Centerline
2-in. piece
Waste slot with ¼-in. bit, clean up with chisel.
Scribe line slightly larger than card.

Fig. 3: Dividing the center assembly

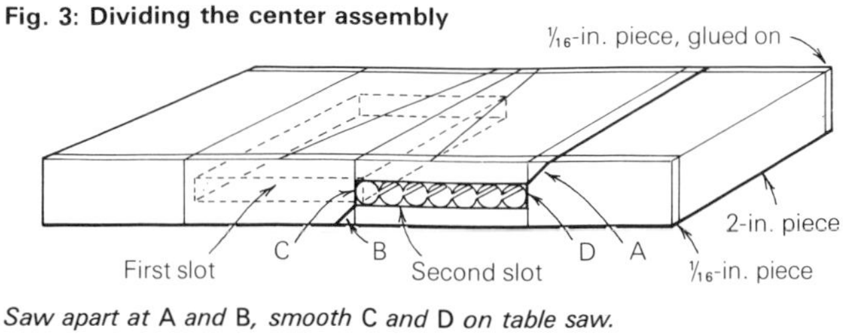
1/16-in. piece, glued on
C
B
D
A
2-in. piece
First slot
Second slot
1/16-in. piece

Saw apart at A *and* B, *smooth* C *and* D *on table saw.*

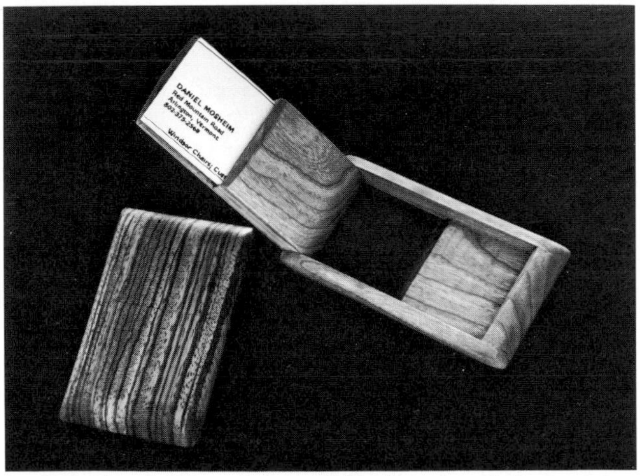

Cook Neilson

Precise sawing, boring and gluing yield a box whose design can adapt to other purposes. These are of zebrawood, left, and cherry.

Fig. 4: Locating the dowel hinges

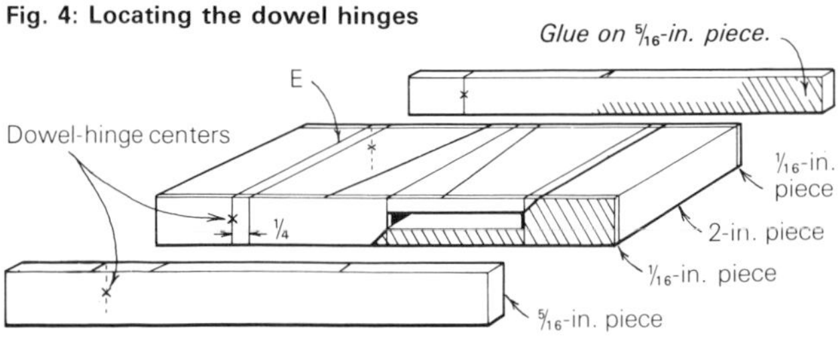
Glue on 5/16-in. piece.
E
Dowel-hinge centers
¼
1/16-in. piece
2-in. piece
1/16-in. piece
5/16-in. piece

Wooden Eyeglass Frames
Making a spectacle of yourself

by Howard Bruner

My original motivation for carving a pair of eyeglass frames was economic as well as aesthetic. The first pair was native walnut reclaimed from a trophy base. I started with the basic shape of my metal aviator-type frames, exactly duplicating the inner dimensions to fit my lenses. From there I added a nose-straddling eagle linked to a bear, a weasel, a rabbit, a squirrel, an owl and the profile of a native American—all on the faceplate. One temple had a dragon breathing fire, the other an organic motif.

Although wearing such flamboyant spectacles never fails to provoke extreme reactions, carving your own frames can be rewarding. I've worn wood on my face for eight years now, and I think that anyone with a flair for individuality will find wooden eyeglass frames stylish and practical. Wood has been used for eyeglass frames almost as long as people have been putting lenses in front of their eyes to improve sight, and it remained an alternative material until the Industrial Revolution. Considering the many attractive wood species currently available, and the high cost of metal and plastic frames, wood is worth taking seriously.

The wood you choose is critical. It must be strong and even-grained. I have used walnut, Oregon myrtlewood and iron bark. I found walnut to be a little heavy and brittle. Oregon myrtlewood solved the weight and breakage problems as well as being, from my experience, one of the finest carving woods available. Iron bark is a shipwrights' choice for railings and other exposed areas on ships. This wood is heavy and oily, somewhat like teak. Its worst characteristic is a tendency to check and warp. My latest frame design called for an exceedingly strong, dense wood, so I picked iron bark to produce the pair I wear now.

The faceplate—The faceplate must be shaped according to critical dimensions (figure 1). The distance between the bridge edges of the lenses (D.B.L.) and the pupillary distance (the distance between pupils, dead center) are extremely important. It is best to work with an optometrist, if you can find one interested in the challenge. There is also the parabolic curve and the panascopic tilt to be considered. The first is the shallow curve across the faceplate from temple to temple. It is slight but important for accurate positioning of the lenses in relation to the eye. The panascopic tilt is the vertical angle between the plane of the lenses and the temples. This varies from 72° to 80°. Lastly there is the base curve of the lens, the curve of its outer face, which determines the shape of the rabbet the lens fits into. I gauged the critical dimensions from the metal originals on the first frames I made, and faked them on my second and third attempts.

You can make the frames first and then have the lenses dimensioned and ground to fit, but it's not easy to find a creative optician willing to do this sort of work. It's easiest to have the lenses ground first and then to carve the frames using the lenses as templates. I have found two ways to make the frames, and will describe both.

One-piece frames—The simplest method is to carve the entire faceplate from a solid piece of wood. But because the sides of the frames are short grain and thus liable to crack, the

Fig. 1: Eyeglass frames

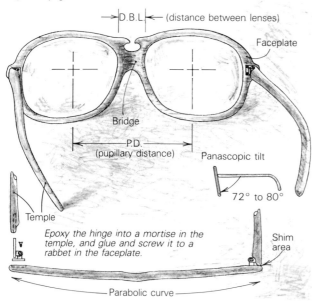

→|D.B.L.|← (distance between lenses)

Faceplate

Bridge

P.D.
(pupillary distance)

Panascopic tilt

72° to 80°

Temple

Epoxy the hinge into a mortise in the temple, and glue and screw it to a rabbet in the faceplate.

Shim area

Parabolic curve

Fig. 2: Alternative construction, a joined faceplate

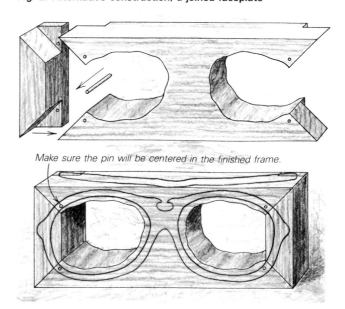

Make sure the pin will be centered in the finished frame.

From *Fine Woodworking* magazine (July 1983) 41:68-69

Rough out the faceplate, sawing the outline and the curve across the face from temple to temple. Then cope out the lens holes and carve the lens rabbet, test-fitting often, as above. The rabbets for the temple hinges, below, are chiseled for a neat fit.

Bruner sporting his wooden frames.

lenses themselves must provide structural support. Plastic lenses are best because they add flexible strength to the frames and because they let you use less wood than heavier glass lenses will allow. Heavy frames and lenses have an annoying tendency to slip down on your nose. Until the lenses of a one-piece faceplate are finally cyanoacrylated into place, the frames must be handled gingerly.

The first woodworking operation is to rough out a design in the faceplate blank. I bandsaw the outline with a narrow blade, and cut the inner holes for the lenses with a portable saber saw. A coping saw will work well too. I use an X-acto knife, chisels and files to further define the design. Begin at the bridge, making sure the fit on the nose is comfortable before turning to the lens area. Setting the lenses in rabbets on the inside of the faceplate is the most demanding part of the project. Work from the bridge toward each temple, carving the rabbet to conform to the shape of the lens, not only its outline but its face, or base curve. The quality of the glue bond depends on uniform contact with the frame around the entire lens. It is also critical that the lenses not be tilted vertically in relation to one another.

Lap-mitered frames—To avoid the disadvantages of having weak short-grain on the sides of the frames and of having to rely on the lenses for strength, you can make the two frame sides from long-grain members. These are joined to the faceplate with pinned, lapped miter joints, as shown in figure 2. The critical thing here is that the pins end up in the middle of the final thickness of the frame. Draw the shape of the frames on the blank before locating the pin.

Temples and hinges—When the faceplate is shaped, rough out the temples. Temples have a compound curve where they

hook behind the ear, and it's best to copy the shape from another pair of temples you already know to be comfortable. If you do not have a model, you can use cardboard templates. In thin sections, wood loses its elasticity, and in time the temples may begin to fit loosely, requiring an adjustment. My solution is to mortise the metal hinges (pirated off a pair of plastic frames, but also available from an opticians' supply house) into the temples and to rabbet them into the faceplate. This allows minimal play and enough clearance to shim between the frame and temple when necessary. Another problem is the fit over the nose. Leave a little extra wood in the bridge, making final adjustments with fine files and razor knives, or with sandpaper.

Before mounting the lenses, sand and finish the frames. I've used polyurethane, the only problem with which is on the nose saddle, where skin oils and perspiration are concentrated enough to break down the finish.

Durability is affected by grain orientation, species of wood and the quality of the joints. Wood was originally rejected in favor of stronger, more consistent materials suitable for mass production. Anyone willing to create a pair of wooden frames should be prepared to treat the investment with care, because they are breakable. But remember, too, that they are usually repairable. My history of wearing wood is crowded with smashes and fractures. In one of the more memorable instances, a bus literally ran them down. Dodging traffic, I gathered all the pieces—the lenses, miraculously, were hardly scratched—and with patience and epoxy I had them on my face again in two hours. Frames of the other commonly used materials would not have been repairable at all. □

Howard Bruner is a professional woodworker in Astoria, Ore. Photos by the author.

into the front leg. Then cut the mortises in the front leg. There is a ½-in. shoulder at the top of the tenon—which leaves some wood at the top of the corner post for strength—but there is no shoulder at the bottom. I begin with an undersized bit in my drill press, being careful not to get too close to the lines, and not to go so deep that the brad-point will leave marks at the bottom of the finished mortise. (I don't like to leave any machine marks on my reproductions, even when they will be hidden.) I complete the mortise with chisels prior to mitering the front tenons on the aprons, which I cut a little short so they don't touch inside the mortises. As a final touch, I undercut the shoulders a little so that the face of the apron will. draw up snug to the post.

Now we come to the interesting part, the joinery at the back legs, which is shown both in figure 3 and in the exploded drawing. The two front aprons are mortised to the back legs at 45°. There are two back aprons, one of which carries the hinged leg.

Cut the inner back apron to length (notice that this piece has no tenons). Then cut the hinged apron, leaving it about 8 in. overlong for the time being, and make the hinge. It is much like the hinge of a Hepplewhite card table, but there are a few noteworthy differences. It has a built-in stop at 64½°, and to make this work, the hinge pin must be offset more than half the board's thickness from the end. This leaves some extra wood to bear against the inner apron, as shown in the hinge details in figure 3. Final fitting of the stop is done by trial and error before the hinge strip is glued to the inner back apron.

As also shown in figures 2 and 3, there is an end block at each end of the hinged apron. One of these blocks is the fixed part of the wooden hinge, and the other can be made from the excess length of the hinged apron. It is by means of the end blocks that the back-apron assembly is tenoned to the legs. There is some careful fitting to be done before gluing up this assembly. First mortise the back legs and cut the tenons on the end blocks, then fit the hinge together. Next bandsaw the left-hand end block so the hinged leg can nest

into it (see the photo below if this sounds confusing). You can use the leg template to determine the profile of the curve.

Now glue the end blocks to the inner back apron, but don't glue on any legs yet. As you can see in figure 2, the hinged leg's corner post must first be half cut away so the leg can swing under the inner back apron. Work on the mortise-and-tenon joint at the hinged leg until everything fits, paring back the shoulders on the hinged apron's tenon so that the leg ends up in exactly the right nesting position. Finally, glue up the back-apron assembly, including the hinged leg but not the others.

Now on to the angled mortise-and-tenon, which is not nearly so difficult to make as it may look. First the tenon: I set a sliding bevel to the angle shown on the plans, then transfer it to the top and bottom edges of the apron blank—I always mark such lines with a knife, since pencil lines are too fat to be accurate. Then I simply bandsaw close to the lines and pare down to them with a chisel, as shown in the photo below.

The mortise is a little trickier, but not

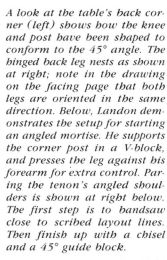

A look at the table's back corner (left) shows how the knee and post have been shaped to conform to the 45° angle. The hinged back leg nests as shown at right; note in the drawing on the facing page that both legs are oriented in the same direction. Below, Landon demonstrates the setup for starting an angled mortise. He supports the corner post in a V-block, and presses the leg against his forearm for extra control. Paring the tenon's angled shoulders is shown at right below. The first step is to bandsaw close to scribed layout lines. Then finish up with a chisel and a 45° guide block.

really difficult. You can pre-drill most of the waste by supporting the corner post in a V-block as shown. Using the drilled holes as a guide, pare the mortise to full width with chisels. You can protect the very thin area at the inside corner from splitting off by using the 45° guide block, just as when cutting the tenons.

With the joinery cut, it is time to bandsaw the curves on the aprons. The pattern is centered on the apron and extends as far as the tips of the knee blocks, as shown in figure 4. After bandsawing the curves, remove the sawmarks with a rasp and chamfer the inner edges with a knife or chisel. The original table shows rasp marks clearly, and the ⅜-in. wide chamfering is a series of very bold cuts.

Glue the table together upside down on a flat surface, and when it is dry, rub on the interior glue blocks. The front angle on the original table was 88½° instead of 90°. I am not sure whether this was deliberate, so that the table would fit into a corner even if the room were slightly off-square, or whether it was just one of those things that happens. My table is also 88½°, and if you choose to follow the plans exactly, yours will be, too.

Now bandsaw the knee blocks and glue them on—but notice that the back knee block on the left rear leg must be relieved, as was done with the end block, so that the hinged leg can nest inside it. Bandsaw the relief cut before gluing on that knee block. Also notice that the forward-facing knee blocks at the back legs are larger than the others so they can meet the posts at a 45° angle. They must also be cut from slightly thicker stock, but these differences will be obvious when it comes time to make the blocks.

Reshape the tops of the knees on the back legs as well as the knee blocks to fair them back to the apron. Finish shaping the outsides of the back corner posts at the same time. Next chamfer the outside corners of the front leg and the hinged leg, then go ahead and make the top.

I cut the top's molded edge with an ogee plane and a hollow plane, but if you don't have these you can begin by cutting a shallow rabbet and then finish up with files. The notches are cut with bandsaw and chisels.

There is a curious joint where the leaf folds. It is not quite a rule joint, nor the tongue-and-groove that might have been found 50 years earlier, but rather a more delicate nesting rabbet-and-bead that does not conflict visually with the notched corners, whether the leaf is up or down. I

made mine with old planes, but any method will work. Pay particular attention to the location of the hinge pin, which determines how the leaf will align with the top in both the hanging and upright positions.

I attached the top with rubbed glue blocks and nails, the same method used on the original. This allows no provision for seasonal wood movement, and you could fasten your top differently if you'd like. Some old pieces eventually split, and some did not. My table, in fact, has a nice small split already, which I welcome as a sign of age. The original's top, ironically, is still fine after more than two hundred years.

I don't like to think of it as faking, but you could say that my table aged a little faster than the original. I added some wear marks where the original table had them, then eased the edges with a Scotch-

Brite pad. I smoothed the bottoms of the feet by rubbing them with a brick, duplicating the moving around that the original must have experienced in its lifetime. For the finish, I applied a home brew of green walnut husks steeped for a month or so in water. This helps darken Brazilian mahogany so that it looks more like the Cuban variety used by 18th-century cabinetmakers. I sealed this with a brushed coat of thin shellac. Five or six subsequent shellac coats were padded on, with some dry pigments mixed in to achieve a semitransparent patina. I took off the gloss with some 0000 steel wool, and everything came together at once. Suddenly there were two old tables side by side, a gathering of the rarest of the rare. □

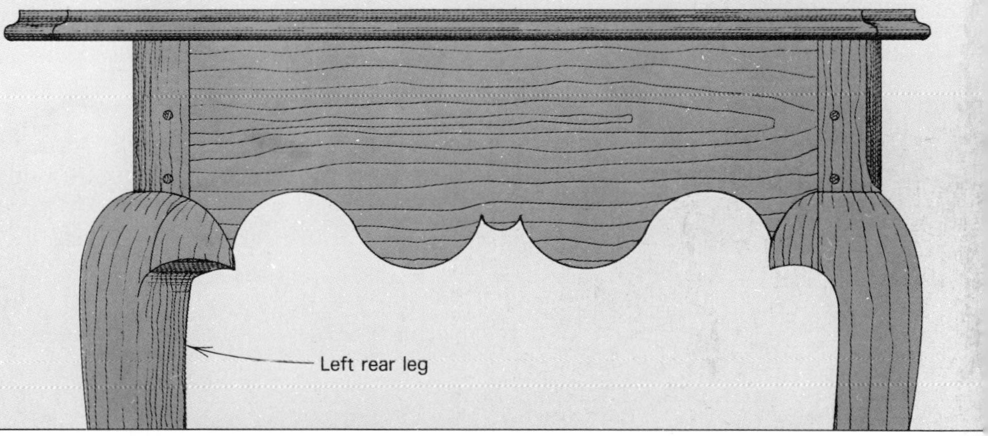

Gene Landon restores antiques and makes period reproductions in Montoursville, Pa.

Fig. 3: Posts, aprons and hinge

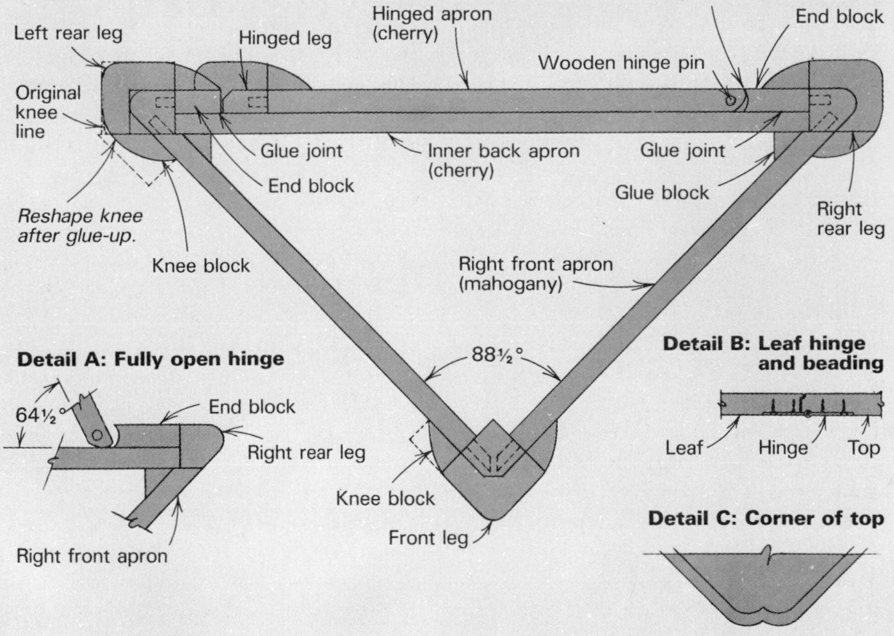

Left rear leg · Hinged leg · Hinged apron (cherry) · Hinge closes without gap. · End block · Wooden hinge pin · Original knee line · Glue joint · Inner back apron (cherry) · Glue joint · End block · Glue block · Right rear leg · Reshape knee after glue-up. · Knee block · Right front apron (mahogany) · 88½° · Right rear leg

Detail A: Fully open hinge

64½° · End block · Right rear leg · Right front apron · Knee block · Front leg

Detail B: Leaf hinge and beading

Leaf · Hinge · Top

Detail C: Corner of top

Fig. 4: Apron detail

Left rear leg

Adirondack Chair
A fresh look at an old favorite

by Bruce Beeken and Jeff Parsons

Inspired by Vermont artist Janet Fredericks' painting of two old Adirondack chairs (top left photo, facing page), the authors designed their own updated version of this popular outdoor chair. Its straightforward construction lends itself to short-run production.

For nearly a century, the familiar Adirondack chair has been a part of the north-country landscape. The classic version of these carpenter-cobbled chairs consisted of nailed-together pine boards that were usually given a coat of leftover house paint. Owing to joinery that didn't accommodate wood movement, many Adirondacks soon worked themselves into kindling. Nonetheless, the chair's simple and pleasing form has ensured its popularity as an outdoor chair.

Our interest in the Adirondack chair began several years ago, at a time when we were identifying our shop's emerging goals. We were interested in designing a functional, solid-wood object suitable for short production runs. An exhibit by Janet Fredericks, a local artist whose paintings of rural Vermont life include images of Adirondacks, catalyzed the project. The chair was ideal. It satisfied our requirements and provided us with an opportunity to

improve an already appealing design. The north country had contributed to our aesthetic sensibilities; by building an improved Adirondack chair, we could reciprocate and enjoy that landscape in comfort.

The first Adirondack was built by a Westport, N.Y., man in the early 1900s. It is said that he gathered his family on their lakeside lawn, where he mocked up chairs to test both seat and back angles, searching for a combination that would make the chair's flat boards comfortable. Shortly thereafter he patented the "Westport Chair," which, though popular, was notoriously uncomfortable. Despite this shortcoming and the chair's vulnerability to the weather, the design has proved to be aesthetically durable.

Our chair began at the drawing board. Using the comfort lines described in *Basic Design Measurements for Sitting* (Agricultural Experiment Station, Univ. of Arkansas, Fayetteville, Ark. 72701,

Photo this page: Didier Delmas

Old Adirondack chairs were fastened with rust-prone nails, a shortcoming the authors improved with mechanically sound joints and shipbuilders' trenails.

Janet Fredericks

Fig. 1: Updated Adirondack

Angled, housed slip dovetail

Housing is angled to accommodate side-piece splay.

Slip dovetail

Pin is angled to allow for arm rake.

90°

Front leg

Dry splines join back.

Two-piece back is mortised into lower back.

Trenailed mortise-and-tenon

Lower back

Side piece is trenailed into notch in front leg.

Side piece

Arm

Front leg

A jig sampler

Jig making, which comprised a large part of our Adirondack chair project, underlies the success of most production runs. The chief function of a production jig is to orient the wood blank so that the part can be reproduced precisely and safely. For efficiency's sake, a jig must suit the movement of both operator and machine. Orientation of joints means that many parts must be made as lefts and rights, thus left and right jigs are often required.

We designed three basic kinds of jigs to make the 16 wooden parts for our chair: jigs for profiling, tapering and joint-cutting. The photos and drawing offer a glimpse into our approach to jig making.

The chair's curved parts—the arms, side pieces and back—were made with a series of shaper profiling jigs. Two of the arm jigs are pictured in the photos at the top of the page. The jigs themselves mimic the specific part's shape. After the blank is bandsawn to within ⅛ in. of the finished profile, the part is mounted and both jig and part are passed through the shaper. The jig's edge guides against a bearing that is part of the shaper's knife collar, and the knives crisply cut the profile in much the same way that a router flush-trim bit works with a template.

Versatility can reduce the number of jigs needed. The six seat slats, for example, were all beveled on the shaper using one jig adjusted to each slat's different bevel angle by a plywood template. Often, though, clamping and machine limitations make one jig impractical. A single jig wouldn't do the arms for us because grain direction and anchor points for the

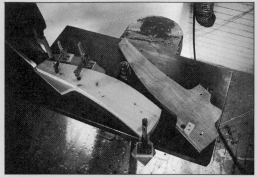

The chair's curved parts were produced with shaper profiling jigs such as the two shown for the arms, above left. Two were needed for each arm because clamp anchor points keep the jig from being fed past the knives in one continuous motion. Parsons, above right, has bandsawn a rough arm blank and is shaping it to the final profile with the first jig. He'll mount the part in the other jig to finish the job.

By tapering its arms and legs, the authors gave their Adirondack a lighter, more refined personality, while leaving enough wood for strong joints. Above, Parsons feeds the arm-tapering jig through the planer. The arm is tapered in three passes by raising the bed after each cut.

The authors' tablesaw doubles as router table, and the fence shown also does double duty. Above, Beeken uses one side of it to mill an angled dovetail pin for the chair's front-leg-to-arm joint. By reversing the fence, he can rout the straight pin for the lower back.

bulletin 616), we developed overall proportions and the shapes and appropriate cross sections of the joined parts, at the same time considering how each part could be jigged for production. At this stage, it was important to introduce design changes without compromising the character that had first drawn us to the chair.

Functionally, an outdoor chair must be comfortable for extended periods of lounging. The sitter must have enough room to stretch, shift position, or curl up with a blanket. The original Adirondack had a fairly narrow seat and wide, horizontal armrests that tended to be unsympathetic to the elbows. We solved this problem by introducing a wider seat, sweeping curves on the inside edges of the arms, and a sloping arm. The original chair's back-to-seat angle was harsh, and the low-slung seat (6 in. off the ground) made getting out difficult. Seat height should make exiting the chair a simple affair, so we raised it slightly and applied a reverse curve for comfort. The curve also keeps the occupant's back from being jammed into the back/seat intersection and the knees from being clipped by the seat's front edge.

Traditionally, Adirondack chairs were nailed together, sometimes with galvanized fasteners. The problems that such fasteners present when exposed to water are well known to boatmakers. Water wicking along the fastener into the wood causes rapid deterioration. Moisture also swells the wood, and when the wood shrinks with drying, the fasteners become loose, turning the chair wobbly. White cedar's ability to resist rot made this preferred boat material an obvious choice for our chair.

We eliminated metal fasteners entirely, substituting interlocking joints with good mechanical strength at each stress point (figure 1), p. 79. The seasonal stress and movement about the yard to which an outdoor chair is subjected call for stout joinery at key locations, namely where the arms join the front legs and where the lower back joins the upper back and the side pieces, so we used mortise-and-tenons and slip dovetails here. To provide enough material for sound joinery, we made these components out of 6/4 stock. Where possible, we tapered the thick parts—in both length and width—to avoid visual clumsiness.

From *Fine Woodworking* magazine (May 1985) 52:46-49

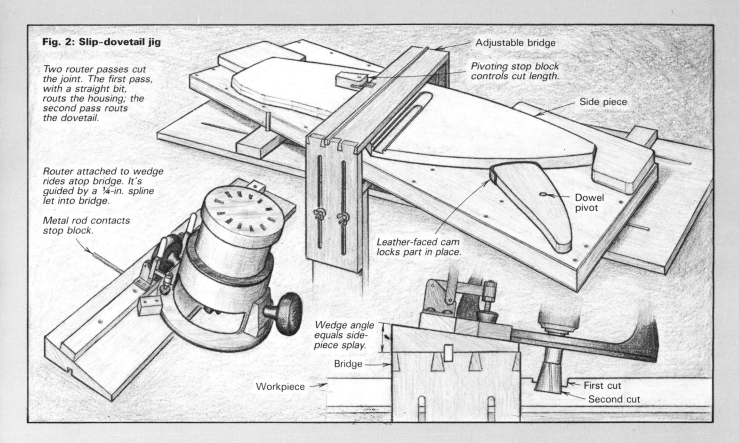

Fig. 2: Slip-dovetail jig

Two router passes cut the joint. The first pass, with a straight bit, routs the housing; the second pass routs the dovetail.

Router attached to wedge rides atop bridge. It's guided by a ¼-in. spline let into bridge.

Metal rod contacts stop block.

Adjustable bridge

Pivoting stop block controls cut length.

Side piece

Dowel pivot

Leather-faced cam locks part in place.

Wedge angle equals side-piece splay.

Bridge

Workpiece

First cut

Second cut

clamps prevent it from being passed by the spindle in one continuous motion. Double-spindle shapers and different mounting techniques can solve this problem. We have a single-spindle shaper, however, which spins counterclockwise. This requires jigs sympathetic to grain direction, and shaping must be done from both faces.

To give our chair a lighter, more refined look, we tapered the arms and legs in both width and length. This leaves wood where it's needed for strength and joint making,

while removing it where it isn't. The bottom left photo on the facing page shows the taper jig we built to mill the compound tapers. The jig bases are torsion boxes, which are lighter and more stable than solid wood or plywood and much easier to build compound angles into.

Probably the most involved jig is the one for the angled, housed slip dovetail that joins the lower back to the side pieces. (figure 1). In tapering the side pieces, material is removed from one side only, which encourages them to warp. By hous-

ing the dovetail (which is canted to match the angle of the side pieces), we avoided a lot of exasperation in fitting.

Routing the pins for the slip dovetail was simpler. By having the bottom of one of our tablesaw's extension wings machined flat and parallel to the top, we are able to bolt a router under the wing so the saw doubles as a router table. The bit projects through a hole bored in the wing. We clamped an angled fence to the wing, then milled the pins by feeding the stock vertically past a dovetail bit.   —B.B., J.P

Where strength wasn't as important, we pinned the parts with trenails (pronounced "trunnels"), traditional shipbuilding fasteners that are really large wooden nails. Trenails are easily turned on the lathe, but we needed two dozen per chair in two sizes, so we found it more economical to buy them from Kisly Systems Inc. (18 Pearce Ave., Manasquan, N.J. 08736). After dipping the rot-resistant locust trenails in marine epoxy, we drove them into tapered, counterbored holes in the joined parts. Shipbuilders leave their trenails proud, flushing them up later with a sharp slick. To avoid cleanup on the finished chairs, we turned a domed head on our trenails and let them project slightly.

After drawings were completed (and the jigs shown on the facing page were designed), we made a prototype, which allowed us to figure production time and provided us with a sales tool. By multiplying the prototype production time by our hourly shop rate, we were able to establish a basis for pricing the chair. To test our business acumen, we presold enough chairs to comprise a run, printed a spec sheet and included a photograph of

the prototype, then sent about 30 flyers to prospective clients, architects and gallery representitives. This resulted in enough sales to proceed with the first run of 18 chairs, a number sufficient to test our economics yet small enough to minimize potential losses. When the last chair was delivered, a review of our figures revealed that a modest 5.5% profit remained after materials, overhead, labor and sales commission.

The chair project proved rewarding in several ways. We delighted in transforming large stacks of live-edged white cedar into symmetrical piles of parts. Learning new production methods introduced us to briskly paced teamwork, and the accurate record-keeping we devised advanced us into realistic business practices. The chair's success was all the more satisfying because we managed to improve a traditional design while producing a piece appropriate to our shop and its surroundings.   □

Bruce Beeken and Jeff Parsons are graduates of Boston University's Program in Artisanry. Their shop is in Shelburne, Vt.

Adjustable Drafting Table
A prize from palletwood

by Roger Sherman

Lumber prices getting you down? Did you know that those ragged-looking shipping pallets piled up down at your local machinery dealer are made from a wide variety of hardwoods from around the world? I made the drafting table shown here from pallets and other discarded odds and ends. It sits in my shop, demonstrating to potential clients that skill and imagination can turn even the humblest materials into something worthwhile.

The table's dimensions are flexible; make it larger or smaller according to your requirements and available materials. Though the thickness of the parts isn't critical, make paired parts (the two trestle uprights, for example) the same thickness.

To make the top, I butted together two sink cutouts from Formica kitchen countertops and glued them to a ¾-in. plywood backing. I beveled the joint between the Formica pieces before assembly, then filled it with automobile body putty. A single piece of countertop or plywood might cost more but be less work.

From shipping pallet to trestled frame, the red oak of Sherman's drafting table now supports a Formica top, not freight.

The top trim and the stand are red oak, and the knobs on the adjustment bolts are waste circles from holes I'd cut out for a wine rack. To prevent the prongs on the T-nuts from splitting the wood, I hammered them over and epoxied the nuts in place. The slide's bottom crossbrace is through-dovetailed to the slide uprights; the upper brace is attached with a stopped, sliding dovetail. The trestle uprights are haunch mortise-and-tenoned into the feet, while the trestle brace, which serves as a footrest, is lap-joined to the trestle uprights. The dragon is the symbol for adversity, so I carved dragon heads on the ends of the brace, enabling me to keep my foot on adversity while working.

The top is attached to the slide with heavy, 6-in. strap hinges, brazed open at 90°. Alternatively, you could use ³⁄₁₆-in. thick strap iron, heated and bent to shape. Each hinge screws to the top and is attached by two bolts to the slide upright. The top bolt is a pivot; the bottom bolt rides in a slot, which permits adjustment of the tabletop's tilt. Slots in each slide allow for adjusting the table's height. I routed the slots, but you could make them on a drill press.

As for pallets, most are made of oak or poplar, but I've also seen willow, ash, beech, locust, hickory, holly, butternut, maple and cherry. Pallets from Asia, Australia and the Orient are generally oak, mahogany or a mishmash of hardwoods. You can get pallets almost anywhere, but avoid those from chemical warehouses, oil refineries, drug companies, insecticide manufacturers, fertilizer plants or any other place where you have no knowledge of what the pallet carried. Chemical residues on a pallet can be very harmful to your health. Department stores, tile outlets (you'll find foreign pallets), automobile and motorcycle distributorships, discount stores, air-cargo terminals, rail yards, piers, ship terminals, fruit and vegetable sellers, and furniture and appliance stores are a few of the safer sources.

You can salvage 90% of a pallet's wood if you're careful taking it apart. First cut the slats from the stringers, then use a prybar with the claw facing you to extract the nails. I've found that only prybars made of flat stock will work; I've had no luck with cat's paws, crowbars or pinch bars. Be sure to wear gloves and eye protection—pallet nails are usually case-hardened and their heads can snap off suddenly. Stubborn nails, or ones with missing heads, can be coaxed out with a pair of carpenters' pincers. Plug the nail holes, and most of the time you won't notice where the nails were.

The pallet, if tamed, is a friendly beast, and the two of you can spend an enjoyable time together with mutual benefit. □

Roger Sherman designs and makes furniture in Baltimore, Md. Photo by the author.

From *Fine Woodworking* magazine (May 1985) 52:64-65

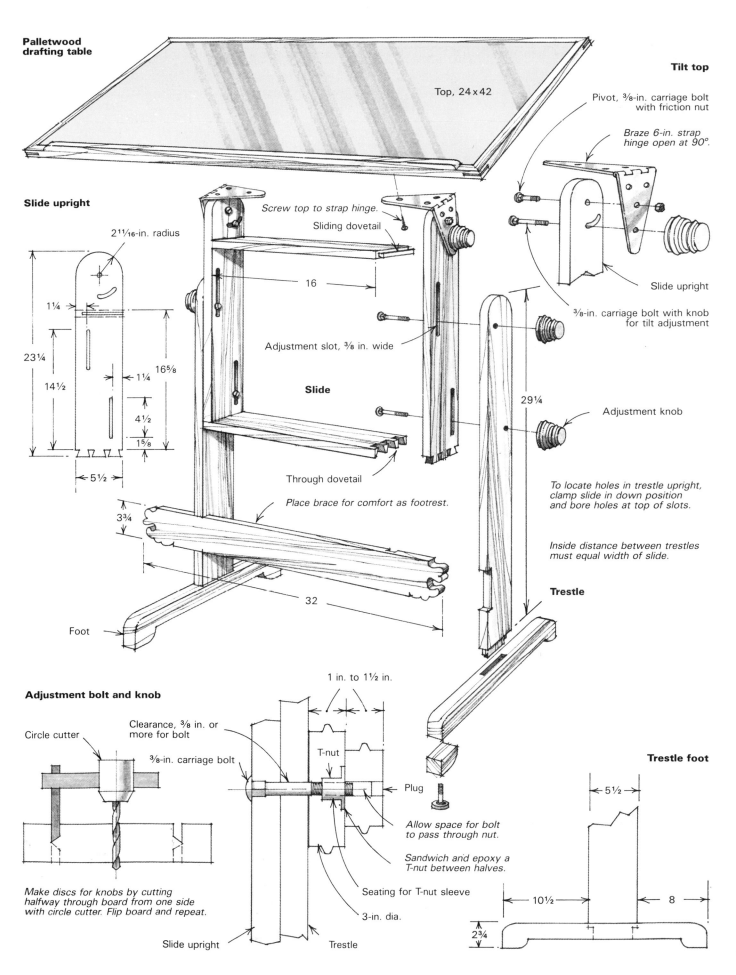

Palletwood drafting table

Top, 24 x 42

Tilt top

Pivot, ⅜-in. carriage bolt with friction nut

Braze 6-in. strap hinge open at 90°.

Slide upright

2¹¹⁄₁₆-in. radius

Screw top to strap hinge.

Sliding dovetail

16

1¼

23¼

14½

1¼

16⅝

4½

1⅝

5½

Slide upright

⅜-in. carriage bolt with knob for tilt adjustment

Adjustment slot, ⅜ in. wide

Slide

29¼

Adjustment knob

Through dovetail

Place brace for comfort as footrest.

To locate holes in trestle upright, clamp slide in down position and bore holes at top of slots.

Inside distance between trestles must equal width of slide.

3¾

32

Trestle

Foot

Adjustment bolt and knob

Circle cutter

Clearance, ⅜ in. or more for bolt

⅜-in. carriage bolt

1 in. to 1½ in.

T-nut

Plug

Allow space for bolt to pass through nut.

Sandwich and epoxy a T-nut between halves.

Seating for T-nut sleeve

3-in. dia.

Make discs for knobs by cutting halfway through board from one side with circle cutter. Flip board and repeat.

Slide upright

Trestle

Trestle foot

5½

10½

8

2¾

Drawing: Joel Katzowitz

Two Sleds

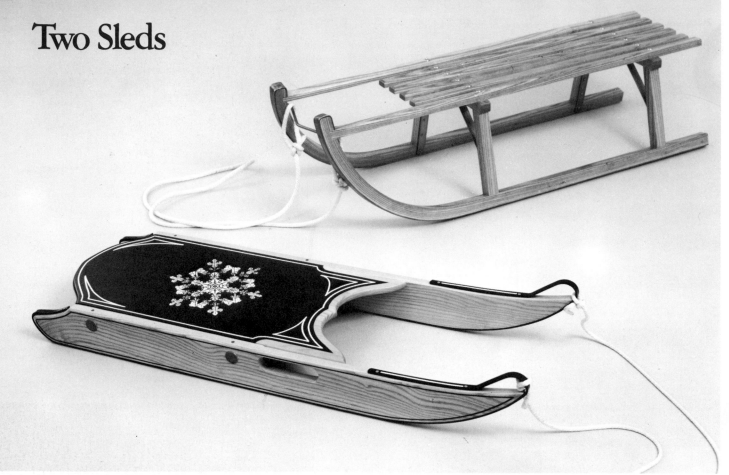

To survive a breakneck dash down a snowy slope, a sled's structure must be robust but relatively light, criteria met by both designs pictured here. Jonathan Shafer's Austrian sled, top, has laminated runners buttressed by steel underpinnings. John Sollinger's simpler hardwood clipper, below, was inspired by traditional 19th-century New England designs.

Shiny paint dresses up Vermont clipper

by John Sollinger

I'd been employed as a full-time woodworker for most of my life and the work had always been satisfying. But ever since my wooden-model building days in grade school, I had always wanted my own shop. Yet I never knew quite what direction my design and building efforts should take. One day about six years ago, my wife suggested I stop talking about it and actually do it. She even had the product: wooden sleds.

Because I live in snowy Vermont, sleds have always been objects of wonder and beauty to me, natural enough, I suppose, from an object that earns its keep toting firewood and groceries yet can still carry passengers on a heart stopping joyride down a steep slope. The design inspiration for the sled shown here came from a couple of magazine articles describing styles of sleds produced in this country during the past century and a half. Substance was added to the style when a neighbor took me on a private tour of the nearby Shelburne Museum's collection of antique sleds and sleighs. The photographs, dimensions, and notes on construction details taken from the sleds at the museum led us to choose the hardwood clipper as our first sled project.

I began three sizes of clippers and finished the smallest in time for my daughter's first Christmas in 1980. An enthusiastic reception encouraged us to establish the Vermont Sled Co. We

later added a rocking Holstein cow and some smaller items, but the sleds remain my favorite product. The clipper is handsome, simple and extremely rugged, all of which make it ideal for small-shop production. It's composed of five pieces of wood—a frame consisting of two stretchers tenoned into two runners and a seat or platform whose chief function is to keep the sledder from falling through to the snow, but which also strengthens the frame. The sled's real strength lies in the pinned tenons that join the stretchers to the runners. It's an attractive detail and capable of surviving the constant pounding sleds must endure. Since the runners are fixed, you steer by dragging a heel or toe (depending on riding position) on the side you want to turn toward.

The drawing on the facing page shows construction details. Dimensions can be scaled up or down for any desired size or function. Our sleds range from 32 in. long by 10½ in. wide to 45 in. long by 13 in. wide. Our largest sled, the Long Rider, has a slatted seat and the runners are pierced for lightness and looks. We use ash for the runners, sugar maple for the stretchers, white pine for the seat and hardwood dowels capped by mahogany plugs for pinning the tenons. The runners are shod with mild steel bar stock, available at hardware stores. The sleds are finished with a clear satin-finish polyurethane and

From *Fine Woodworking* magazine (November 1985) 55:56-59

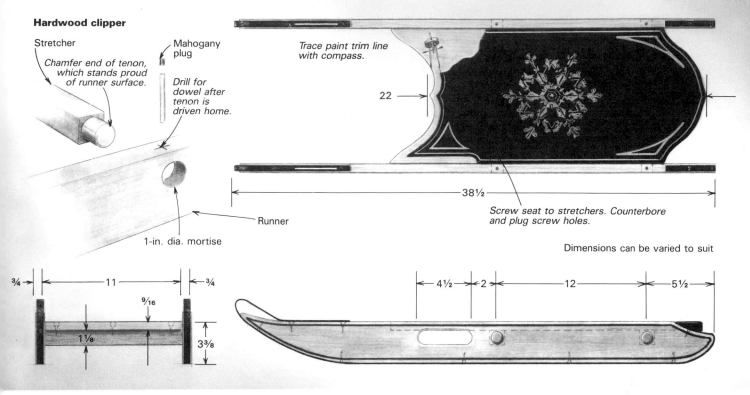

Hardwood clipper

Stretcher

Chamfer end of tenon, which stands proud of runner surface.

Mahogany plug

Drill for dowel after tenon is driven home.

Runner

1-in. dia. mortise

Trace paint trim line with compass.

22

38½

Screw seat to stretchers. Counterbore and plug screw holes.

Dimensions can be varied to suit

¾   11   ¾

9/16

1⅛   3⅜

4½   2   12   5½

An extra runner, left, serves as a bending form for the sled's steel shoes. Bent cold, the steel is coaxed with a hammer where overbends are required. To paint the seat, Sollinger masks with tape to layout lines struck with a compass. Once the enamel has dried, he paints pinstripes with a striping wheel guided by hand or, where practical, a straightedge.

over that I spray a high-gloss exterior enamel for color.

Select a board for the runners wide enough to lay out both, top to top—that way color and figure will match. For obvious structural reasons, avoid checks or knots. We bandsaw the runners out of 4/4 stock before thickness planing and we use a pattern to guide final profiling on the shaper and overhead router. All sanding, except final touch-up, is done at this time using a pneumatic sander. Round mortises for the stretcher tenons are drilled after sanding, to keep the edge of the hole from rounding over, ensuring a crisp joint. We cut the stretcher tenons with a chucking tenoner that produces a 1-in.-dia. tenon with a square shoulder, however, you could just as easily turn the tenon on a lathe. Tenon length should be ⅛ in. longer than the thickness of the runner so it will stand proud of the runner's surface. Before assembly, we chamfer the end of the tenon on a disc sander to produce a nice decorative touch.

Pine for the seats is glued up then planed to 9/16 in. before being bandsawn to shape. We glue and screw these seats cross grain to the maple stretchers which is, strictly speaking, not good construction practice. However, we have had no problem with cracking because we avoid checked or figured wood and glue up only when the humidity is in the 40% to 60% range.

That way the seat will neither shrink nor swell enough to cause problems. If you are concerned about the seat cracking, you could skip the glue and fasten it with screws through slotted holes, but the sled will not be as strong. You could also make a slatted seat instead of a solid one.

Once the sled is assembled and sanded with 220-grit paper, you can finish as desired. We apply a coat of satin polyurethane (made by Zip-Guard), let it dry, sand with 220-grit, then spray a final coat. If you don't have a spray rig, brushing will give acceptable results. We use satin polyurethane because it's easy to apply and the enamel for the seat adheres well to it. For the seat's glossy finish, we use an oil-based enamel called Lustaquick made by Kyanize in Everett, Mass. 02149. Local paint stores can order this material and it is worth the wait. The paint has a high solids content and whether sprayed or brushed, it produces a beautiful, durable finish in one coat.

We mask the sled, spray the main color area and, when it has dried, paint the pin stripes with a striping wheel (from Brookstone Co., 127 Vose Farm Rd., Peterborough, N.H. 03458, catalog number 2812, $11.75 in 1985, or from auto-body supply stores). Practice with the wheel before tackling the sled. Good results can also be had with an appropriate-sized sword-striper brush, thinned paint

Things to Make   **85**

and a steady hand. The snowflake pattern on the seat is taken from a book by W.A. "Snowflake" Bentley, a Vermont farmer who photographed thousands of snowflakes as a hobby during the 1930s. We had a silk screen made to transfer the pattern. For just one sled, you could make a paper stencil and paint it by hand or hand letter a child's name as we are frequently asked to do.

To complete the sled, add steel shoes to the runners. The shoes are of ⅛-in.-thick by ½-in.-wide mild steel, cold bent around a form made from an extra runner screwed to an 8/4 pine base. I added hold downs and bumps where overbending is required to counteract the steel's natural springiness. Mild steel is flexible enough to take sharp bends without breaking and it drills easily. Before bending, we bore and countersink for the screw holes and grind off the flash. The steel is placed in the jig and pulled around, using a hammer and wood block to coax it into the tighter curves. Once bent, it's finished with a rustproof primer and a high-gloss enamel finish coat. Screw the shoes on, add a suitable length of rope and your sled is ready for use.

Our three original sleds have seen four Vermont winters. They're left outside from the first good ground cover (usually November) to the last possible day we feel they can still be used in late March. Off-season storage is in the rafters of our barn where the temperature and humidity reach rather unpleasant extremes. They get rained on, climbed on and generally abused. These sleds are tough and have far exceeded our expectations for usefulness and fun. We fully expect them to become valued possessions of our grandchildren. □

With his wife, Sharron, John Sollinger operates the Vermont Sled Co. in North Ferrisberg, Vt.

Austrian design has laminated runners   by Jonathan Shafer

One of my fondest childhood memories is of the Christmas I received a wooden wagon with removable sides. After many years of driving it with one leg out for propulsion, hauling people and things and using it as a saw horse in the yard, the wagon was retired to the garage while I finished growing up. I have since rescued the wagon, cleaned it up and built new removable sides. The project gave me the urge to create something unique for my own son, an object that would be worth rescuing from my garage someday. So, with my son's joy of the outdoors as apparent as my desire to graduate from straight-plane woodworking, I built an Austrian sled, based on a picture I saw in an L.L. Bean catalog.

As the drawing on the facing page shows, the sled has a slatted seat attached to a pair of frames that join the runners. The runners themselves are laminated using the form shown or, if you prefer, they can be steambent. In either case, you'll need to construct the bending form, as well as the jigs to cut the angled mortise and tenons that hold the frame together. The bending form should be made longer, both vertically and horizontally, than the runner so the laminae can be clamped to it. The excess runner length is cut off later.

I laminated the runners out of white ash but any species with good bending characteristics and straight grain will do, such as the oaks or hickories. I made my laminae ¼ in. thick so only four were required for each runner. Laminae this thick may have a tendency to spring back and if this becomes a problem, use thinner strips. If you soak the wood in hot water first, it will bend easier, but then you must clamp the strips in the form and let them dry overnight before gluing. I used epoxy glue for the runners, which, in addition to being waterproof, is good at filling any small gaps between the laminae.

The mortises in the runners that accept the uprights were cut on a shop-built horizontal router table (you could, of course, use a commercial table). So the sled will have good torsional strength, the uprights are splayed out 13°, requiring angled mortises where the uprights join the seat crosspieces. I devised the router mortising jig shown in the drawing to cut the angled mortises. I cut the tenons for the uprights on the tablesaw, using a dado blade and with the miter gauge set to 77°. To position the shoulder cuts precisely, I fastened a board to the miter gauge then clamped a stop block to it, referencing each shoulder cut against the stop block. If you don't have a dado blade, cut the tenons with repetitive passes over a regular blade, then clean up the cheeks with a sharp chisel.

After a dry run to check the fit of all the joints, glue the two uprights into each seat crosspiece using the fixture illustrated. Before applying clamp pressure, square the frames by measuring diagonally from the upright/crosspiece intersection to the inside of the crosspiece shoulder, adjusting the frame until the measurements are equal. When these joints have cured overnight, use the same fixture (move the cleats to accommodate the runner) to glue the uprights into the runners.

The seat, or deck, is composed of six slats. The two outermost ones are wedged-shaped in section and are let into an open mortise in the top inside edge of each runner. I found it easiest to mark the slat's cross section right on the runner then saw and chisel the mortise by hand. However, I didn't glue the exterior slats in place until after I'd fitted the steel runner caps so that I could butt the steel tightly against the wood. The four interior slats are rectangular in section but their edges are radiused with a ¼-in. roundover bit. All of the slats are attached to the crosspieces with flathead brass woodscrews and decorative washers.

Finish up by attaching frame braces, a tow bar and steel caps to the runners. The frame braces are of ⅛-in.-thick steel, ¾ in. wide and the runner caps are the same steel, 1 in. wide; the tow bar is a ¼-in.-dia. rod. Since I didn't have access to a forge, I cold bent the steel where possible. However, to bend the caps sharply around the tips of the runners, I heated the steel to a cherry-red glow in a barbeque grill then bent it around a wooden block identical to the runner's cross section. I also heated the ends of the tow bar and flattened them with a hammer to yield a better bearing surface where the bar contacts the runners. The metal parts are attached to the sled with countersunk wood screws. Three coats of Deft Exterior Clear Stain #2 polyurethane, applied over wood and metal parts, completed the project. □

Jonathan Shafer lives in Columbus, Ohio, where he works in the construction industry. The commercial version of the sled is made by Paris Manufacturing Co. in South Paris, Maine.

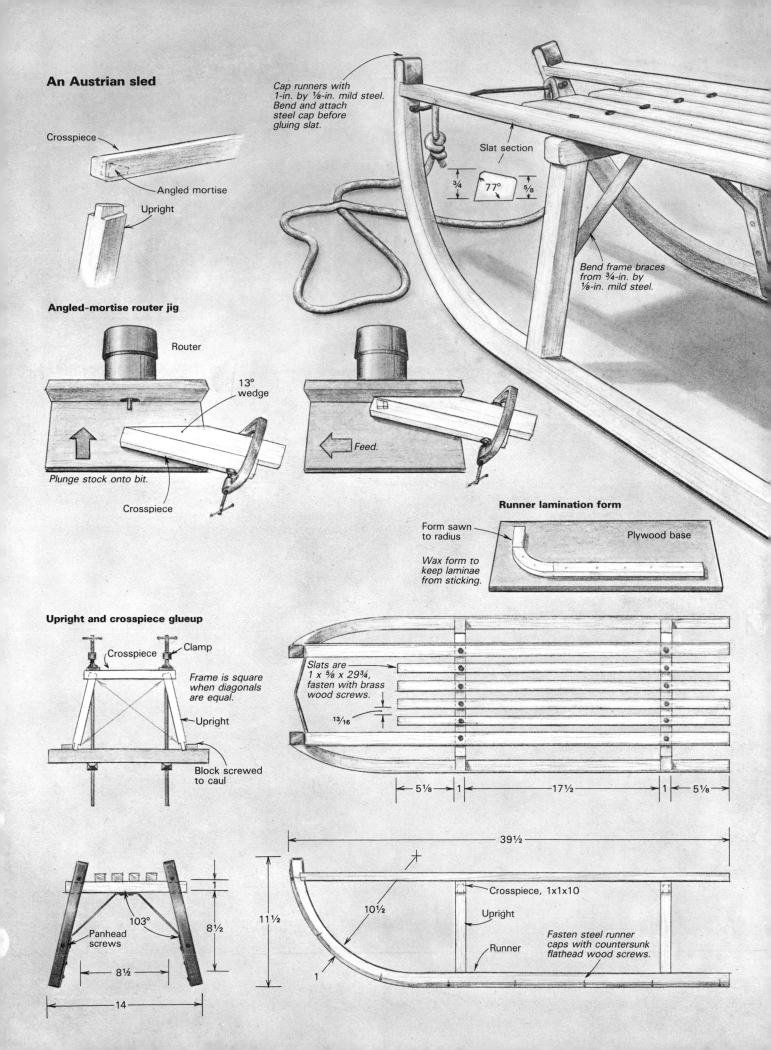

An Austrian sled

Crosspiece

Angled mortise

Upright

Cap runners with 1-in. by ⅛-in. mild steel. Bend and attach steel cap before gluing slat.

Slat section

¾

77°

⅝

Bend frame braces from ¾-in. by ⅛-in. mild steel.

Angled-mortise router jig

Router

13° wedge

Plunge stock onto bit.

Crosspiece

Feed.

Runner lamination form

Form sawn to radius

Plywood base

Wax form to keep laminae from sticking.

Upright and crosspiece glueup

Crosspiece

Clamp

Frame is square when diagonals are equal.

Upright

Block screwed to caul

Slats are 1 x ⅝ x 29¾, fasten with brass wood screws.

13/16

5⅛ | 1 | 17½ | 1 | 5⅛

39½

Crosspiece, 1x1x10

Upright

Runner

Fasten steel runner caps with countersunk flathead wood screws.

11½

10½

1

103°

Panhead screws

8½

8½

1

14

Sculptural Inlay
Three-dimensional images in wood

by Nancy H. Bolstad

Allen used bone and natural wood colors, not stains and dyes, to create dragon inlay.

Carved rose picture has bloodwood blossoms, imbuya leaves, maple background and walnut frame.

Two years ago my husband and I were beginning to market our new series of limited-edition jewelry boxes when we saw some eyecatching three-dimensional wood pictures by Tom Allen. Unlike conventional marquetry images created with veneers, these pictures, which Allen calls "sculptural marquetry," were made by combining shaped pieces of wood up to 1 in. thick. We were impressed with the designs and craftsmanship, and knew that these sculptured pictures would look good on our boxes, replacing our frame-and-panel lids. Soon afterward we began working with Allen, and together we have produced a series of boxes featuring floral motifs, such as the rose box shown above.

Basically, to create these inlaid pictures, Allen rubber-cements three or four boards of different species together to create a multicolored stack. Then he bandsaws through the stack following a pattern cemented to the top board and pulls the laminated pieces apart. This produces four copies of his pattern, each of which resembles a monotone jigsaw puzzle. By combining parts from the four puzzles, he can produce a colored version of his original pattern. These colored parts are then carved and drum-sanded until they blend together into a flowing, three-dimensional picture. Each picture develops from one of Allen's own drawings of a real-life object or scene, from a photograph, or from patterns in carving and stained-glass design books. His favorite pictures depict the mountains, forests and other nature scenes around his home in Silverton, Oregon.

Before cutting any wood, Allen refines and simplifies his sketches to make a pattern. Very fine details that cannot be cut without breakage are eliminated. Then the entire picture must be divided into even-sized parts to compensate for wood lost to the bandsaw kerf when the picture is cut out—if the pieces differ markedly in size, the proportion of shrinkage might be too high in one part of the picture, creating an unpleasant distortion. Finally, the curves of each piece must be adjusted so that none is smaller than the ¼-in. radius the blade can cut. When Allen is satisfied with the pattern, he copies it—the copy will be cemented to the laminated blank, the original goes in his design file.

Each of the boards is planed and thicknessed, then it's cut to the overall size of the complete picture, plus ½ in. to ¾ in. all around to allow for shrinkage caused by cutting and carving the pieces. Grain pattern and figure must be carefully considered. Horizontal grain is best for sky, for instance, and some boards suggest clouds or textures like hay. Although the thickness of boards in the stack varies from design to design, the pieces of wood chosen for the background and foreground of a floral picture generally are about ⅛ in. thick; for leaves and stems, about ¼ in. to ⅜ in.; and for blossoms, about ¾ in.

For gluing the boards together, Allen prefers rubber cement because it's strong enough to hold the stack together but yielding enough to allow him to easily pull the cut segments apart later. After attaching his pattern to the top board of the glued-up blank, he saws the stack on a 1940s vintage 12-in. Craftsman

From *Fine Woodworking* magazine (March 1985) 51:66-67

bandsaw with a fine-cut ⅛-in. blade. It's important that the blade be carefully tensioned and aligned, because if it wanders or is not square to the saw table, the pieces from the top of the stack will not fit with the bottom pieces. Allen doesn't have any set order for cutting out the parts, but he works with pieces large enough to be held safely. For a relatively small piece, he'll cut it out together with one of its larger neighbors, then hold the larger piece while sawing the small piece free.

Once the pattern has been bandsawn, Allen separates the pieces, retaining those with the colors he needs for a particular picture and discarding the rest. He rubs off the rubber cement, then fits the picture together as tightly as possible on his workbench, knifing or sanding off any rough spots or projections during this preliminary fitting. The bandsawn edges will be further refined as they are fit into the frame, which is prepared by routing out a ⅛-in. deep rabbet into a box, hand mirror, tabletop, cradle, cabinet or other piece of furniture.

To fit the inlay into the frame, Allen begins with the largest outside piece and trims it to fit against the edge of the rabbet. Then he adds an adjacent piece and some interior pieces, and proceeds around the edge, trimming and sanding the parts to fit in place. If a section has to be drastically altered, he bandsaws it again. Otherwise, he works with X-acto knives and drum sanders. Often the last piece or two needs more trimming than the others.

The picture is complete at this stage, but relatively flat. To create the flowing lines and curves that give the illusion of a real flower or landscape, Allen now shapes each piece by pushing it against motor-driven 80-grit sanding drums. He controls the cutting effect of the drums by varying the way he holds and moves each piece and by using different-size drums. Constantly moving the piece as it's being sanded produces a rounded, soft effect, while holding the wood in one position produces a faceted or scooped-out area. A 2-in. dia. drum is good for shaping large pieces and making shallow facets, and a 1-in. or ¾-in. dia. drum takes care of deep scoops, small facets and tight curves. Needlenose pliers are real finger-savers when sanding small pieces.

After finish-sanding the shaped pieces with 150-, 220- and 400-grits on the drum sanders, Allen dry-fits the picture once again to make sure all the pieces look right. Then he coats the rabbet with 1-hr. epoxy darkened with a little lampblack to make any slight discrepancies in fit less noticeable. He's careful to make the epoxy layer thick enough to bed the pieces and to ensure a good bond, but not so thick that it squeezes up between the individual pieces. Painstakingly laying each piece in place, he usually does the larger background pieces first, then moves on to the smallest pieces, using tweezers where necessary. After the epoxy has hardened, he brushes two or three coats of tung oil on the picture and the frame to preserve the wood and its colors, wiping off the excess oil between coats. When the tung oil is dry, he applies paste wax and buffs the entire piece with a soft brush.

Allen and his wife, Deborah Warren, produce 400 to 500 inlays each year in their business called "Joy of Doing." In Allen's words, "There is certainly a joy in building something with your hands. And it is exciting to see my drawings brought to life by the woods I choose. It is incredible how much each different wood affects the picture. I can control it a little, but the wood is unpredictable and adds its own surprises." □

Nancy H. Bolstad is co-owner of Bolstad Woodworks in Willamina, Ore.

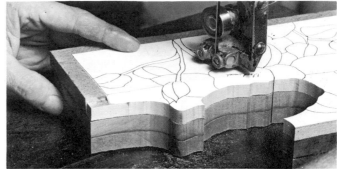

To make an inlay, rubber-cement naturally colored boards together, then bandsaw around your pattern, pull the stack apart and pick the appropriately colored pieces. Be sure the saw is perfectly aligned, or parts from different boards won't fit together.

Picture parts are shaped on 80-grit drum sanders before they're inserted into a frame. Cut deep scoops, small facets and tight curves on a small 1-in. dia. drum mounted on a benchtop motor (above). Larger drums create gentler curves and shapes. The mountain forest inlay shown below features stars of silver and a moon cut from bone.

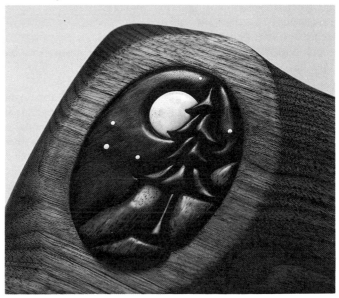

Photos top and center, this page: Curtis Almquist; bottom right and p. 88: Ralph Gabriner

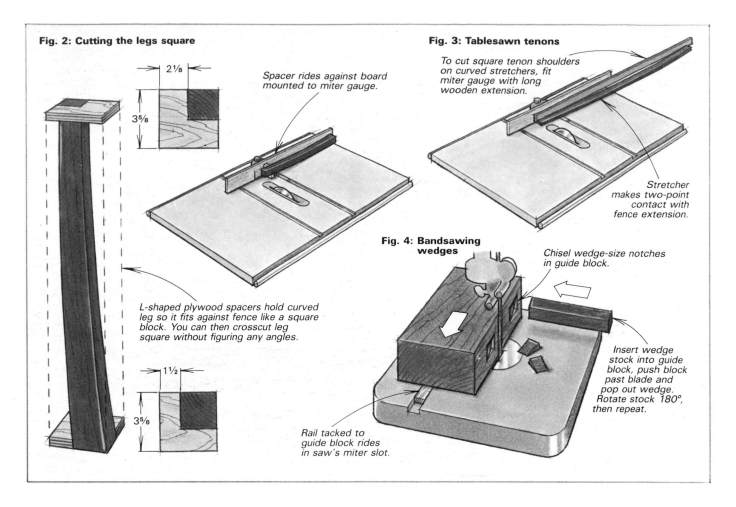

Fig. 2: Cutting the legs square

2⅛

3⅝

Spacer rides against board mounted to miter gauge.

L-shaped plywood spacers hold curved leg so it fits against fence like a square block. You can then crosscut leg square without figuring any angles.

1½

3⅝

Fig. 3: Tablesawn tenons

To cut square tenon shoulders on curved stretchers, fit miter gauge with long wooden extension.

Stretcher makes two-point contact with fence extension.

Fig. 4: Bandsawing wedges

Chisel wedge-size notches in guide block.

Insert wedge stock into guide block, push block past blade and pop out wedge. Rotate stock 180°, then repeat.

Rail tacked to guide block rides in saw's miter slot.

saw, using two homemade L-shaped spacers (figure 2) that hold the end of the leg against the miter gauge and parallel to the saw table so the leg can be crosscut. I cut the ⅜-in. by 1-in. mortises with a hollow-chisel mortiser attachment for a drill press. The mortises must be cut from the outside face of the leg because that's the only way the piece will lie flat on the drill-press table. If you don't have a hollow-chisel mortiser, chop the mortises by hand. Next notch the bridle joint in the top of the legs by standing the leg upright in a tenoning jig and clearing the ⅝-in. by 1¼-in. slot with a dado cutter. Even though the stretchers are curved, you can cut the tenon shoulders on the tablesaw. Mount a long wooden extension on the saw's miter gauge (or use a large sliding table) and hold the piece face-down with the concave curve facing the extension to cut the first shoulder (figure 3). Then flip the piece to the other side of the blade to cut the second shoulder. Cut the tenons ¹⁄₁₆ in. to ⅛ in. too long—you'll trim them flush after assembly. After cutting the shoulders, stand the stretcher in a tenoning jig and cut the cheeks.

The narrow top and bottom tenon cheeks and their shoulders are bandsawn. I cut the shoulders about ¹⁄₁₆ in. shy of the line, then use a chisel to pare them flush with the shoulders I previously cut on the tablesaw. While I'm at the bandsaw, I cut two slots, each the width of the bandsaw blade, into the tenons for the ebony wedges, which taper from ⅛ in. to ¹⁄₃₂ in. (figure 4).

After scraping and sanding the base parts, assemble the two ends. You can use bar clamps to pull the joints together, but place them so you can drive wedges into the tenons before the glue hardens. Because yellow glue dries slowly on oily rosewood, I leave the clamps on overnight before trimming the ten-

ons flush. To complete the base, glue and clamp the tenons of the lower front and back stretchers into the mortises of the two ends. Be careful not to overtighten the clamps, or you'll bow the stretchers. The base is now rigid enough that you can position the top stretcher over the legs and scribe where the stretchers must be notched to fit into the leg. After cutting the ⅜-in. deep notch, I glue the pieces together and attach the cross supports as shown in figure 1.

I begin the top while the base is clamped and drying. Even though each leaf is really three separate panels held in a frame, I press one large sheet for each leaf, then cut it apart to ensure that the grain pattern will match on all three. I usually bookmatch two long, wide sheets of rosewood veneer for each side of the leaves. Since both sides are so visible, I use show veneers on both, with the flatter, "swirly" grain in the center and the more striped grain to the outside.

To joint the veneer, clamp two sheets between two heavy squared-up boards. Set the sheets so the mating edges protrude ¹⁄₁₆ in. to ⅛ in., then hand-plane the edges flush to the boards with a jack plane or a jointer plane. Next remove the veneer from the boards and tape the mating edges in two stages, first stretching 3-in. strips of masking tape across the seam on the inside face to pull the joint tight, then flipping the veneer sheet over and securing the face-side seam with veneer tape. Remove the masking tape before pressing the veneer. After preparing veneer for each face of the leaves, select a smooth, flat sheet of ½-in. thick Baltic birch or other high-quality plywood for the substrate. Cut these sheets 1 in. oversize all around and with the grain running across

Photos, pages 90-91, Jack Russell; drawings, David Dann

the short dimension. This makes the panel more stable, since the veneer grain continues the plywood's crossbanding, with the grain of each layer at 90° to the next layer.

I press the veneer with 16-in. 2x4 battens over four ½-in. thick chipboard cauls cut the same size as the plywood. Set two cauls on a pair of sawhorses and cover them with waxed paper to prevent the veneer from sticking to the chipboard. Put the veneer face-down on the waxed paper, roll a coat of urea-formaldehyde glue onto one side of the plywood panel and put the glued face onto the veneer. After rolling glue onto the top side of the plywood, put the second veneer sheet, this time face-up, on the plywood. Add another sheet of waxed paper and two more cauls to complete the package. Place the 2x4s in pairs, one on top of the package and another directly below it underneath the panel, and lightly clamp the sandwich together. Tighten the clamps, beginning in the middle of the leaf to squeeze out excess glue. The next day, unclamp the panels and use a handscraper to remove the dry veneer tape and to smooth both faces.

A tongue-and-groove joint holds the panels in the frames. Mill the frame pieces about ⅟₁₆ in. thicker than the veneered plywood and slightly longer than their finished dimensions. Then, on the tablesaw, cut a ³⁄₁₆-in. groove into the inside edge of each piece. After cutting the intermediate rails to length, leaving enough for a tenon on each end, saw the veneered plywood to width, then into the three panels. Rout a centered tongue on the four edges of each panel and on the ends of the intermediate rails.

To assemble the top, arrange the pieces on your bench the way they will be clamped. For the outer frame (two rails, two long stiles), begin at one corner, cut the miter joint and clamp it up to mark the next corner for cutting. Once the second miter is cut, repeat the process for the third corner, and so on. I reinforce each miter with a screw. Before gluing the pieces together, I mortise a shallow ⁵⁄₁₆-in. square hole in the outside edges of each miter, then drill through the mortise for the screw. This allows me to cover the screws with square plugs that complement the table's angular look. If you've accurately cut the three plywood panels, you shouldn't have any problem clamping the leaf into a perfect rectangle. Then screw the miters together and plug the holes.

Planing the frame pieces flush to the veneer is difficult, especially at the corners—it's easy to tear the edge of a rail or stile or to nick the veneer. I plane in from the outside edges with a jack plane or a smoothing plane, using the veneered surface as a register for the nose of the plane to ensure that the frame pieces remain flat. I partially round the outside edges with a ½-in. quarter-round router bit set so that only the lower half of the bit cuts. Then I scrape the entire top and sand with 220-grit. I rout the mortises for the hinges with a template, and hinge the two leaves together. Before attaching the top to the base, I finish the table with at least six coats of clear Waterlox oil.

The three U-shaped brackets holding the top to the base (figure 5) should fit tightly around the crossbraces but still allow the top to slide. If the brackets are too loose, the center of the open table will pop up when someone leans on an edge. Properly installed, the brackets hit the back stretcher when the top is closed and the front stretcher when the top is open. Work out the adjustment by first clamping the brackets in place when the top is closed and moving them around as needed. When you're satisfied, fasten the brackets with round-head brass screws. □

Robert March is a woodworker/designer and head of the woodworking program at the Worcester (Mass.) Crafts Center. Photos this page by the author.

With the veneer sheets clamped between boards so that the matched edges stand proud, March hand-planes the edges.

After joining the veneers with masking tape, March flips the sheet over and props a plank under one leaf to pinch the veneer seam tight. The seam is then secured with veneer tape before the masking tape is pulled off.

Each of the top's two intermediate rails is tenoned into the stiles. Tongues on the three panels slip into matching grooves cut in the table frame.

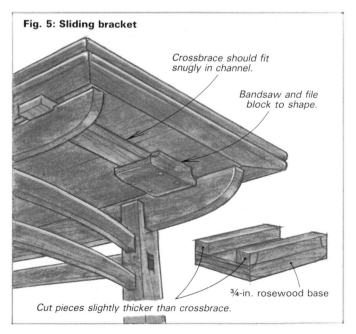

Fig. 5: Sliding bracket

Crossbrace should fit snugly in channel.

Bandsaw and file block to shape.

¾-in. rosewood base

Cut pieces slightly thicker than crossbrace.

Turning Music Boxes
Try a different movement on your lathe

by James A. Jacobson

One of the dilemmas of the turner's craft is the persistent question: What is it for? Over the years, I'd turned innumerable round things, including dozens of boxes and containers, but most of these objects just stood around doing nothing, with no real purpose or function. The question nagged at me. Then one day I turned a little box and fitted a music movement inside. When it began to play, that was answer enough for me.

I've since worked out a variety of shapes and sizes for turned musical boxes. These experiments proved so satisfying that they led me to write a book: *Woodturning Music Boxes.* In this article I'll show you the basics, including how a music movement works (see p. 96), and I'll give a list of suppliers. I'll tell you about my favorite woods, skim over the tools I like, and share some of the turning tips I've picked up. I'll also discuss a shop-made chuck that I find invaluable. Other turners, no doubt, will see ways to apply their own tricks.

Wood—It is my good fortune to live in an area of the Midwest that is endowed not only with hardwood forests, but also with numerous small sawmills, where some of the best wood for turning is almost free for the asking—those pieces that others would consider worthless. I like chaotic and unpredictable grain—sawmill cutoffs from logs, burls and spalted wood.

Some woods transmit musical vibrations better than others, amplifying the sound. Yet in my experience, any wood will make a decent music box. Oak and mahogany, for instance, are said to be poor choices, but when they are turned thin enough, I've found that they work fine. I highly recommend walnut, cherry, hard maple and Osage-orange, but other woods are worth experimenting with. too. Try whatever is in your woodpile—the turned pieces I enjoy the most are from wood that I found, lugged home, and nursed to readiness myself.

In addition to native woods, I've turned music boxes from bocote, padauk and bubinga, though mostly I use these as accent woods for designs on lids, and for decorative plugs: if I have a nice turning block that's flawed, I drill out the flaw and insert a contrasting plug before I turn the piece. Another ornamental, wood-saving trick for a block with one or two major checks is to bandsaw along the check line and glue the block back together with a contrasting piece of veneer between the two pieces.

When working out a new design, I often turn a few prototypes from glued-up construction-grade 2x4s or #3 lumber.

Tools—I prefer scraping tools because they allow me to make very light and precise cuts. This is especially important when turning the soundboard of a music box, the part to which the music movement is attached. The soundboard should be both thin and flat. That way, it not only transmits the music to the air, but also transmits the vibrations to the sides of the turning, for more volume. Musical vibrations will also travel down the sides of a box to the surface beneath. A wooden tabletop, for instance, will amplify the sound.

For rough-turning, especially on larger blocks, I use a 1-in. roundnose scraper, pointed slightly downward. I sharpen it on a 6-in. by 48-in. belt sander with a 100- or 120-grit belt. You don't need a razor edge on a scraping tool. In fact, the edge will cut better if it has a slight burr. To prevent ruining the entire belt, which is used for other things, too, I restrict the sharpening area to a narrow strip along one edge. On smaller jobs, and for lids and insides, I usually begin with a ½-in. roundnose.

I sharpen square and skewed scrapers, which make the finishing cuts, on a regular shop grinder. For the outsides of music boxes, an extra-heavy skewed or squarenose scraper, ⅜ in. thick and 1½ in. wide, is a good tool. I like a long, heavy handle, and often make my own either from hickory or from hackberry. Hackberry, because of its interlocking grain pattern and surface texture, is a non-slip wood and very secure in the hand.

Once in a while I cut rather than scrape, using a long-and-strong ⅜-in. deep gouge. But on the kind of wood I prefer, scraping tools have advantages. A scraper is less likely to tear out unruly grain, and is ideal for truing the walls and soundboard. In addition, a scraper can very cleanly square up the narrow shoulders necessary for lids and for glass inserts.

The glass insert is a clear cover that allows you to watch the movement working yet keeps it clean. I cut my own glass inserts with a circle glass cutter, then smooth the sharp edges on the belt sander. If you'd like an insert but don't want to go to the trouble of cutting your own, you can probably find a replacement flashlight lens near enough to size to do the job. Good hardware stores usually carry them, although these days they're likely to be plastic instead of glass. No matter.

The chuck—When turning a large box, it's best to screw the blank securely to a faceplate, the way you would begin turning any heavy piece of wood. If you want to avoid screw holes in the bottom of the box, use the familiar method of gluing a piece of paper between the block and a wooden faceplate, so that the

Tunesome containers can be made of anything from Osage-orange firewood to choice padauk. The tallest music box in the photo (page 95) is 10½ in. high. The small ones, with single-tune movements, readily sell at craft fairs for about $25 (1984).

From *Fine Woodworking* magazine (September 1984) 48:78-81

How a music movement works

Cylinder music movements were developed by Swiss horologists (watch/clock makers) early in the 19th century. Though designers have evolved some exceedingly complex—and expensive—mechanisms, the basic principles of a music movement are easily understood (figure 1).

Each tooth on a metal comb, when plucked, vibrates and produces a musical note. The teeth are plucked by metal pins on a revolving cylinder, and the arrangement of the pins and tuning of the comb determine the tune. The cylinder is powered by a wound spring, and its speed is regulated by the air resistance of a rapidly whirling, lightweight governor called a butterfly.

In some movements, the on/off switch is merely a wire, called a stopper, that pivots into the path of the butterfly (figure 2A). This makes it simple to adapt most movements to various switches. Wires can be linked to run up through the side of the box to the lid, so the box plays when it is opened and stops when it is closed. Similarly, the stopper can run through the bottom, so the box begins to play when it is picked up. Instead of a wire, I sometimes run a small dowel through the side of the box. My usual stopper consists of a sliding cylindrical weight on a horizontal rod (figure 2B). When you tilt the box to the side, the weight slides free of the butterfly. Tilting the box the other way stops the butterfly.

Some simple movements are made without stoppers—they play until they run down—and some are cranked by hand. A slightly more complicated type of movement plays more than one tune, and usually has a built-in index stop that turns the movement off when each tune is finished (figure 3). These movements are actuated by a sliding switch, and have one clear advantage—the music begins at the start of the tune, not somewhere in the middle. Otherwise, the basic principles remain the same.

Sources: I primarily use Reuge Swiss movements, and these are readily available by mail order. Reuge catalogs its movements according to the number of teeth (the number of notes in the comb) and the number of tunes the movement will play. Reuge's 1.18 movement has 18 teeth and plays one tune. Their 2.36 has 36 teeth—allowing greater range from treble to bass—and plays two tunes. The 1.18 movement will play nearly 3½ minutes on a single winding.

Each movement type is available in a variety of melodies, and many familiar woodworking catalogs (Woodcraft and Constantine's, among others) contain a page of musical movements. In addition to the basic movements that most places sell, you can buy battery-powered movements, miniature movements, and movements with interchangeable cylinders. For the out-of-the-ordinary, try Craft Products Music Boxes, Dept. 95, 2200 Dean St., St. Charles, Ill. 60174; Klockit, Box 629, Lake Geneva, Wis. 53147; Mason & Sullivan, 586 Higgins Crowell Rd., West Yarmouth, Mass. 02673; and World of Music Boxes, 412 Main St., Avon, N.J. 07717. This last source will even make custom movements to play the tune of your choice. There's an organization for aficionados, too: The Musical Box Society International, Box 205, Rt. 3, Morgantown, Ind. 46160.   —J.A.J.

Fig. 1: A simple music movement

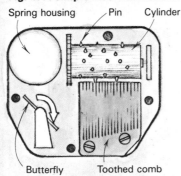

Spring housing · Pin · Cylinder · Butterfly · Toothed comb

The schematic music movement above shows the general principles: A spring turns the large gear on the cylinder, whose pins pluck the teeth on the comb to produce the tune. Speed is regulated by a whirling governor (called a butterfly) powered off the main gear by a gear train (omitted for clarity).

Fig. 2: Types of stoppers

A: Wire stopper

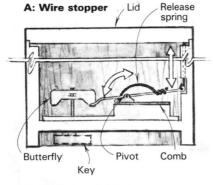

Lid · Release spring · Butterfly · Pivot · Key · Comb

B: Sliding-weight stopper

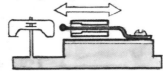

Fig. 3: Automatic shutoff

Cam drops into hole in face of gear at end of tune, pivoting stopper against butterfly.

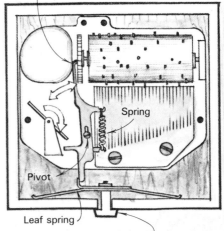

Spring · Pivot · Leaf spring

Switch slides in groove to disengage stopper.

block can be split off later. I bandsaw all blocks round before mounting them. When you have finished as much as you can with the blank on the faceplate, you'll have to reverse the blank so that you can turn a recess in the bottom for the music movement's winding key (and to thin out the soundboard). I've developed a screw-center chuck, shown in the drawing, that holds the box in this position. When trying the chuck, you may find that the center screw doesn't run quite true. It will seem to wobble as the lathe turns. A few gentle taps with a hammer or a wooden block, with the lathe turning, will usually put it right.

Dimensions—The dimensions of a turned music box depend on the size of the music movement. The simple box in the drawing shows the important size considerations, the turning process and some finishing touches. Other ideas can be seen in the photograph on p. 95 and are mostly self-explanatory. All you need to ensure accuracy while turning are some simple measuring tools. Inside and outside calipers and a child's compass are enough, but I like a vernier caliper as well—I usually work in millimeters, because the music movements I use are metric. In addition, I have a gauge for estimating the rounded size of a rough, irregular blank. The gauge is merely a sheet of stiff plastic with concentric circles scribed around a center hole. I position the gauge against the end of the wood, center the largest circle I can, then mark the center through the hole.

Sanding and finishing—For protection, I wear a suede glove on my left hand most of the time when I'm turning, and both gloves when sanding. I back up the sandpaper with pieces of ¼-in. foam carpet padding. These are flexible enough to follow contours smoothly, and they absorb most of the friction heat that would otherwise burn the wood. I begin with 100-grit garnet paper, except on very rough wood, where I use 60-grit. If the paper won't cut the wood fibers with the lathe turning in the usual direction, I reverse the lathe motor for a while, taking care that the faceplate doesn't start to unscrew. Next I sand with 150-grit, followed by 220- or 240-grit. It usually isn't necessary to sand the recess where the movement will be.

For a high polish, I dry-sand with 280- or 320-grit wet-or-dry paper (silicon carbide), followed by 600-grit and a final polish with 0000 steel wool.

I've done my share of shellac-polishing on the lathe, but I have a few reasons for not doing music boxes that way. First, you can't finish the entire piece at one time, because the faceplate or chuck gets in the way. Second, lathe-finishing ties up faceplates and chucks, and on occasion the lathe itself. Third, you sometimes must finish a piece as soon as you've turned it (when remounting it might cause it to go out of balance). I'd rather finish a few pieces at a time, off the lathe, at leisure.

First I apply Watco oil, sanding lightly with the grain with 600-grit wet-or-dry paper to remove the last whiskers of wood. The oil brings out the natural beauty of the wood—I never use stain. When this first coat is dry, I go on in one of two ways: I either apply two or more additional coats of Watco, or brush on a few coats of Deft lacquer, steel-wooling between coats to an even luster. In either case, a coat of paste wax, buffed or rubbed, is a good way to maintain the finish. □

James A. Jacobson, who turns wood in Collinsville, Ill., is currently working on a second book, Crafting Music Boxes. Woodturning Music Boxes *is available from Sterling Publishing Co., Two Park Ave., New York, N.Y. 10016.*

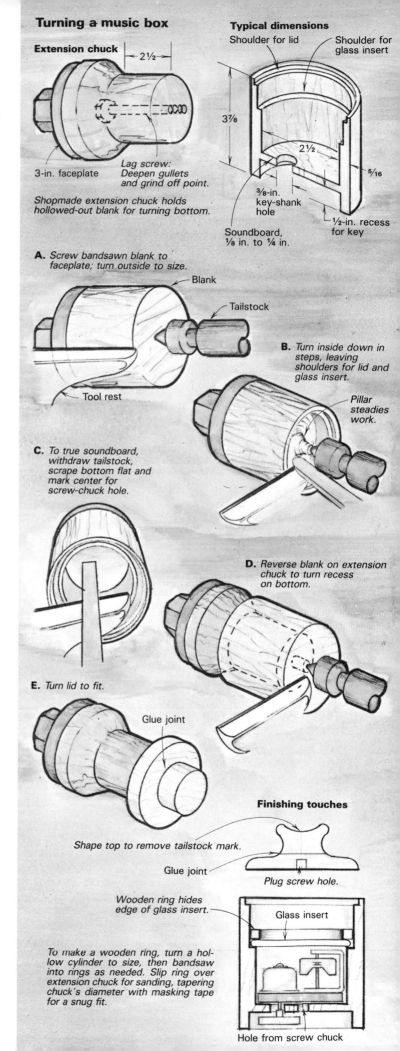

Turning a music box

Extension chuck — 2½

3-in. faceplate

Lag screw: Deepen gullets and grind off point.

Shopmade extension chuck holds hollowed-out blank for turning bottom.

Typical dimensions

Shoulder for lid   Shoulder for glass insert

3⅞   2½   5/16

⅜-in. key-shank hole

Soundboard, ⅛ in. to ¼ in.

½-in. recess for key

A. Screw bandsawn blank to faceplate; turn outside to size.

Blank

Tailstock

Tool rest

B. Turn inside down in steps, leaving shoulders for lid and glass insert.

Pillar steadies work.

C. To true soundboard, withdraw tailstock, scrape bottom flat and mark center for screw-chuck hole.

D. Reverse blank on extension chuck to turn recess on bottom.

E. Turn lid to fit.

Glue joint

Finishing touches

Shape top to remove tailstock mark.

Glue joint

Plug screw hole.

Wooden ring hides edge of glass insert.

Glass insert

To make a wooden ring, turn a hollow cylinder to size, then bandsaw into rings as needed. Slip ring over extension chuck for sanding, tapering chuck's diameter with masking tape for a snug fit.

Hole from screw chuck

Making Room Screens
A wooden hinge for every purpose

by Steven Mackintosh

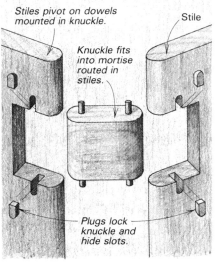

Mackintosh's first screen, left, has a no-show back because slots routed into the frames for the knuckle hinge (drawing above) are visible from the rear.

I don't really know why I got interested in making room screens, since they seem to be the antithesis of the kind of woodworking I'd been doing for several years. I had resolutely tried to design furniture that people would want to *use* every day, not just look at, and a screen is something you can't sit on, store things in or eat dinner at. But after I had made one screen, I found myself making another, and another, and another. Each was an attempt to solve a design problem whose dimensions kept growing with each apparent solution.

Before describing the design dilemmas I found so irresistible, I'd better correct the impression that screens have no practical purpose. They do, although it's not always the reason people buy them nowadays. Before central heating, screens were used to minimize drafts. Today many screens—especially the more highly embellished variety—are purchased only for decoration. Yet they can have functional uses as well, such as shrinking large spaces to more intimate dimensions, providing privacy, hiding clutter, or keeping the cat out of the baby's room without having to close the door. The best use to which I've put my screens is in my booth

at craft fairs. A big screen is a real eye-catcher, and it doubles as a backdrop for some of my smaller pieces, such as a tea cart or a group of music stands.

The spark that ignited the screen-building boom in my shop was Tim Mackaness's article in *Fine Woodworking* on making a wooden screen hinge. This hinge, shown in figure 1, answered the only design problem that had occurred to me at the time: what to do about ugly metal hinges. I had admired Chinese lacquered screens pictured in antiques magazines, but I was puzzled as to why someone would go to all the work of building one, only to limit its aesthetic impact and functional flexibility by installing obtrusive butt hinges. I designed and built my first screen around Mackaness' wooden hinge, using a frame-and-panel arrangement.

I was pretty pleased with that first screen. The overall effect was just what I had hoped for, and the wooden hinges enhanced the design rather than detracted from it, as metal hinges certainly would have done. But the solution to my first design problem instantly revealed three more. The first of these was the issue of "one front and one back side versus two front sides." I had mounted the panels with quarter-round molding, giving the screen a definite front and back. This effect was further emphasized by the hinges, whose pins were let into router-cut slots in the back of the frames. I had carefully filled the slots with matching pieces of wood, but a close look revealed their presence. How much more pleasing and functional, I thought, to have a screen with two presentable sides.

Next was the question of how many panels the ideal screen should have. A screen with two panels is nearly useless, and a three-panel screen is only a little less static. My five-panel original model could assume a couple of interesting shapes, but how about more panels to allow more variety? Finally, there was the matter of price, which I always consider as much a design problem as anything else. The frame-and-panel screen had been pretty expensive, and since hardly anybody *needs* a screen, a lower price figured to be more of an inducement to an impulse purchase.

So, to cut down on construction time, I decided to make the next screen out of solid wood. The result was a nine-panel structure of ¾-in. maple whose design dictated two changes in the hinges. First, I made them much thinner, about ¼ in. rather than 1 in. as on the previous screen. At the same time, I actually increased their strength by making them out of nine plies of veneer. Second, instead of using ¼-in. hardware-store dowels for the hinge pins, I used drill rod sized exactly to the width of the routed slot. To eliminate the screen's "back" side, I let the pins into slots in the edges of the panels, as shown in figure 2. It seemed faster to cut a groove the whole length of the panel's edge with the tablesaw rather than cut individual slots for each pin with the router. Also, the sawblade makes a very unobtrusive ⅛-in. groove in a place that's impossible to see when the screen is unfolded. I filled the grooves with splines, which had to be notched accurately to hold the pins snugly and to keep them from sliding out of their holes in the hinges.

Standing back from the finished product, I was pretty proud of the way I had resolved my first screen's shortcomings. The

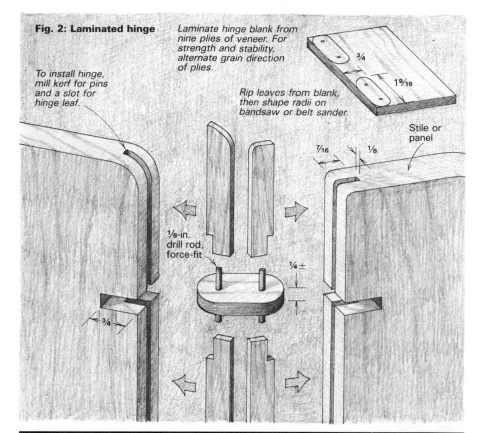

Fig. 2: Laminated hinge

Laminate hinge blank from nine plies of veneer. For strength and stability, alternate grain direction of plies.

To install hinge, mill kerf for pins and a slot for hinge leaf.

Rip leaves from blank, then shape radii on bandsaw or belt sander.

¾

1 9/16

Stile or panel

⅛-in. drill rod, force-fit

7/16   ⅛

¼ ±

¾

Solid-wood panels and a thinner hinge made of built-up veneers let into slots in the panel edges produced a screen equally attractive from front or back.

From *Fine Woodworking* magazine (May 1985) 52:60-63

Things to Make   **99**

A lighter screen with plywood panels called for a new hinge, so Mackintosh designed a knuckle hinge that pivots on dowels (drawing at right). Maple knuckles are let into mortises routed in the panels, then fastened with anodized aluminum interscrews.

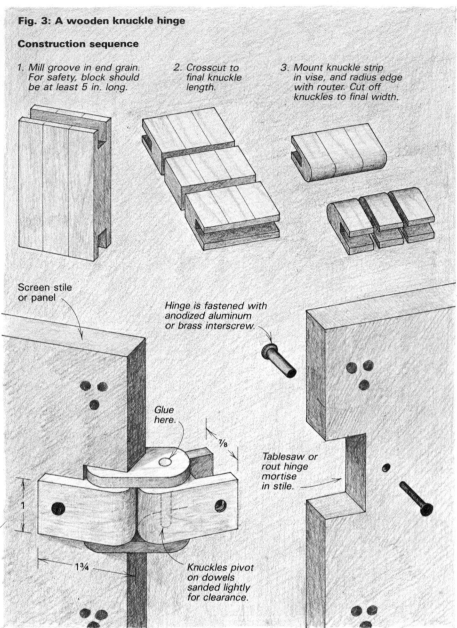

Fig. 3: A wooden knuckle hinge

Construction sequence

1. Mill groove in end grain. For safety, block should be at least 5 in. long.

2. Crosscut to final knuckle length.

3. Mount knuckle strip in vise, and radius edge with router. Cut off knuckles to final width.

Screen stile or panel

Hinge is fastened with anodized aluminum or brass interscrew.

Glue here.

7/8

Tablesaw or rout hinge mortise in stile.

1

1¾

Knuckles pivot on dowels sanded lightly for clearance.

nine-panel screen allowed many interesting configurations, and it had no visually inferior back side. It had also taken a lot less time to make. As a bonus, it seemed much bigger than the first one, even though it was the same height and only about 10 in. wider. Its apparent size, I decided, had more to do with the somewhat monolithic nature of the design. At any rate, it was an imposing presence in my booth, able to catch the eye of even the most jaded craft-show regular.

Almost immediately, however, I began to have product-liability nightmares. Imagine the damage a falling 100-lb. maple wall could do to houseplants, furniture, pets and children, not to mention adults with ambitious lawyers. What I needed was a panel material lighter than solid wood that could hold its shape in 72-in. lengths. There may be some wonderful substance on the market out there somewhere, but the best I could come up with was premium-grade, ½-in. Philippine mahogany plywood, which weighs only half as much per square foot as maple does. The only problem was the untidy look of the edges, which I could solve by painting the screen.

These decisions led me to two more hinge-design variations. First, it wouldn't hurt if the hinges were visually interesting and rather prominent, since the panels were to be fairly plain-looking painted rectangles. Second, the hinges had to be removable so the panels could be repainted. The final version of the hinge, shown in figure 3, can be made quickly using the

tablesaw, router and drill press, and fit into notches cut into each panel's edge with a router, rub collar and template. I secured the hinges to the panels with aluminum interscrews—two-part fasteners consisting of a machine screw that fits into a threaded socket with a slot on its other end. They're sold by stationery suppliers as post-binding screws. To tone down the aluminum, I had the interscrews anodized black at a local plating shop.

As with the previous two screens, when I stepped back to assess what I had done, I had mixed feelings. This one passed several of my tests for screen success. It was nice and lightweight. The hinges, while more obvious than on either of the other screens I had done, still enhanced the

overall design. Best of all, the price was the lowest by far, as long as I didn't get carried away with the painting. But, as before, there was a major drawback I just couldn't get around—the ragged edges of the plywood. I'd thought that painting would hide them, but it didn't really work very well (and I'm not much of a painter anyway). I realized that what I was really after was a system that would allow many readily interchangeable panel treatments—paint, wallpaper, fabric, plain wood grain, wood with inlay.

This called for frames with easily removable panels, and hinges whose attachment method wouldn't interfere with panel removal. To achieve this, I devised the frame method shown in figure 4. I incor-

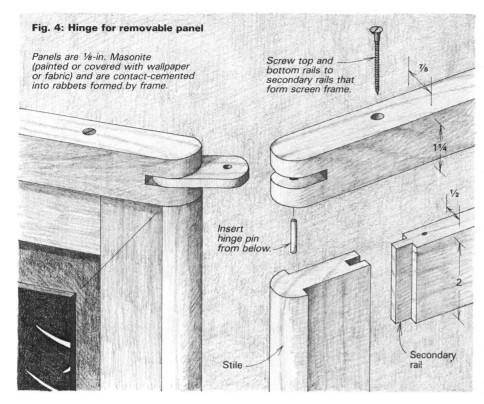

Fig. 4: Hinge for removable panel

Panels are ⅛-in. Masonite (painted or covered with wallpaper or fabric) and are contact-cemented into rabbets formed by frame.

Screw top and bottom rails to secondary rails that form screen frame.

⅞

1¼

½

2

Insert hinge pin from below.

Stile

Secondary rail

Author's lightest screen consists of wall-papered or fabric-covered panels contact-cemented into a cherry frame. The top and bottom rails (drawing at left) are permanently hinged but removable, so the panels can be pried out for re-covering.

A wooden box hinge

by Eric Brostoff

For this pink ivorywood box, Brostoff sculpted the hinges out of ebony.

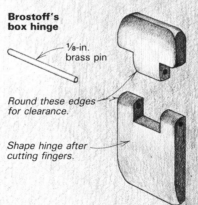

Brostoff's box hinge

⅛-in. brass pin

Round these edges for clearance.

Shape hinge after cutting fingers.

Two years ago I acquired a nearly perfect piece of pink ivorywood, a hard, dense material said to be one of the rarest woods. Native to South Africa, it was once the royal wood of the Zulus. As legend has it, the chief's son had to fashion a spear from ivorywood as part of a ritual signifying his manhood. With such a special piece of wood, I didn't want to make just any ordinary box, so I raided my stash of exotic woods and designed the ebony hinges shown here.

I made the hinges with a box-joint jig on a Shopsmith, cutting a series of fingers, then slicing off sections the width of each hinge. Before I shaped the hinge parts with belt and flap sanders, I assembled the two halves and drilled for the ⅛-in. brass hinge pin, which is held fast with a dab of superglue. You could sand or carve any shape you like, but if the hinge is to work smoothly, the sharp edges of the fingers have to be rounded over a little to provide clearance. The box carcase is African blackwood, which doesn't glue well, so I attached the hinges with epoxy. ☐

Eric Brostoff operates Mountain Top Box Works in Lake Oswego, Ore. Photo by the author.

porated the hinges into show rails that screw into the top and bottom of each panel frame. The frame's structural rails—which are ultimately hidden by the panel and top and bottom rails—are tenoned into the stiles, each of which has a ⅛-in. deep rabbet into which a Masonite panel fits. The Masonite can be covered with wallpaper or fabric, then glued into the frame with contact cement. If you want to change panels, you need only unscrew the hinge rails from one end and work a knife between the frame and the panel. Besides being light, this arrangement has one other important advantage: one side of the screen can have an entirely different treatment from the other.

After all my experimenting with fabric-covered, airbrushed and wallpapered panels, the final incarnation of this screen has ⅛-in. birch plywood panels decorated with colored epoxy inlays. We're using it to cover a door in our living room that we never use. It's doing such a fine job that I don't think I'll try to sell it. Almost a year has passed since I made it, and looking at it every day has made me think a lot about screens. I don't have to justify them to myself anymore, which is a good thing, since I have lots of new ideas I'm going to try. ☐

Besides designing screens, Steven Mackintosh builds furniture in Deansboro, N.Y. Photos by the author.

Spiral Steps

The trick is to make them strong and graceful

by Edward G. Livingston

Trying to describe the innermost workings of the concept and construction of a design, be it a building or a doorknob, is risky business. Risky, primarily because such analysis quite often falls short of explaining thoroughly just what transpired. Risky too, because even though the artist may be doing the explaining, there is a loss in translation between his creative processes and his verbal ones. With that in mind, we would like to take a calculated risk and show the innards of our library ladder.

First, in explaining "why" the ladder: it was created as an experiment. It was the joy of experimenting with the creative process rather than any urgent necessity that triggered the concept. The ladder was a challenge in the functional sense because it was and is a basic instrument used to defy gravity. It is easy enough to get above the ground all right, but how do you get above the ground with a certain amount of grace and aplomb? That is indeed a challenge! A spiral stair, whether it is a full-story size or a partial stair such as a library ladder, provides by its very spiral nature, the intrigue of potential grace and aplomb in climbing. It does in fact beckon to be climbed, so why not enhance this by eliminating as much possible—the extraneous structural supports, for instance—and allow the essence to stand out?

Another large obstacle was solving the actual technical problems relating to fabricating the unit. In other words, "Okay, you have cooked up an idea. Now, how in the world do you build it?"

This part of the conceptual process is extremely important because sometimes it is impossible to translate an idea properly.

A man once said, "Well building hath three conditions — commodity, firmness, and delight." The man, Sir Henry Wotton, was talking about the basics of architectural design, but I like to think that those basics are more universal. I feel that: "commodity" — the function of the design; "firmness"—the structure; "delight"—the aesthetics; are the guts, feathers and all of any of our creative endeavors. Combining Wotton's basics and the intrinsic challenges of the ladder, plus the creative impulse in me, into a physical whole is the sum of the experiment.

The physical aspects of putting together a unit like the ladder are patience, glue, and wood—in that order. The first part of the structure is basically a laminated column with alternate armature laminations left void—thus creating a mortise type of receptacle to receive the tenon type end of the individual riser assemblies. The spiral of the stair is provided by the second set of column wedge laminations, which flank either side of the armature laminations and differ in that their cross section is in the shape of a wedge or pie. The armature laminations are interrupted by the risers. The wedge laminations are continuous for their individual full length. The riser laminations provide a nest for the riser itself, and the wedge laminations lock the riser in the nest.

The second part of the structure is the foot. Its importance and complexity are deceiving. It was also the most difficult of the design features to resolve simply because the total unit required a large stable underpinning which was hard to build without making it look too large and too heavy.

The design was resolved by providing floor support continuously along the same axis as any anticipated applied weight from above. The foot follows exactly the same curve as the treads above. The flow of the curve allows the foot a little respite from weight and size and at the same time provides continuity with the flow of design above. The complexity of the foot exists because of its curve. In order for the foot to have any strength in bending, it has to be cross-laminated so by the time the foot reaches from toe to the heel at the column, there is a stack of six laminations each juxtaposed grain-wise so as to reinforce each other.

The last part of the structure are the tread riser assemblies—simple laminated cantilevers. The risers at the column end are in effect tenons that actually project completely through the column. The only atypical tread riser assembly is the first one at the floor and this because it actually embraces the foot as the foot approaches the base of the column.

Assembly of the total unit can be tricky because the twisting motion the wedges provide makes it difficult to obtain straight line pressure points in applying clamps. Also the wedges themselves have a tendency to pop out of their intended plane as pressure is applied. There is also a problem of keeping track of a needed reference point. Everything about the unit is either twisting or curving, and unless care is exercised the fabricator will be wondering about up from down.

Normally we first glue up the armature pieces, risers included, with a wedge piece added on one side as reinforcing. When these have cured, we then juxtapose the armature-wedge assemblies and glue. This allows for more control of the otherwise slippery wedges. We keep all of the column edges rough at this point to allow for the maximum availability for clamping area. Also in order to keep everything true, i.e., the column vertical and the risers horizontal, we use as a reference point the vertical line made by the take-off point common to all the riser assemblies.

After the column is completed in the rough, the foot

From *Fine Woodworking* magazine (Spring 1976) 2:42-43

assembly is inserted in the slot provided by the lowest riser armature. This armature is then beefed up by two full dimension laminations on both sides to provide adequate glue line support for the incoming foot assembly. This juncture is an important one because it is the point where all the accumulated vertical stresses in the column assembly are transferred to the foot.

With the foot on, the column straight up and down, and the riser armatures poking out in place, the tread side wings can be added. It is best that the side wings be preassembled and sanded because it is a difficult maneuver to get sanding equipment in the tight space between treads after the pieces are assembled.

The one redundant feature of the ladder is the finale or handhold at the top of the column, which is a series of built up laminations of a different wood applied over the column end—a blob of a different wood made integral with the column end.

After the unit is together the column is sculpted with a seven-inch automotive disk sander with 16-grit abrasive, thus providing the continuous flow of the twisted column. From then on it is finish sanding, an oil finish, and a wipe of the brow!

The time involved in fabricating the unit is approximately 40 hours, over half of it devoted to the necessary sanding. The glue used is aliphatic resin and there is no hardware or metal in the structure. The wood is Japanese oak throughout except for the handhold. ☐

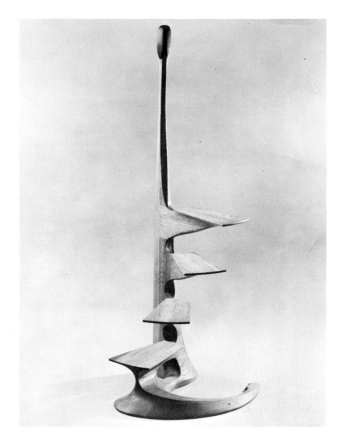

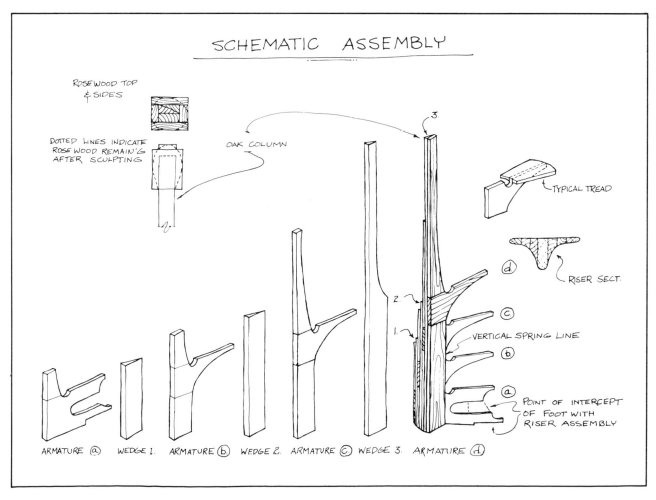

SCHEMATIC ASSEMBLY

ROSEWOOD TOP & SIDES

DOTTED LINES INDICATE ROSE WOOD REMAIN'G AFTER SCULPTING

OAK COLUMN

TYPICAL TREAD

RISER SECT.

VERTICAL SPRING LINE

POINT OF INTERCEPT OF FOOT WITH RISER ASSEMBLY

ARMATURE ⓐ   WEDGE 1.   ARMATURE ⓑ   WEDGE 2.   ARMATURE ⓒ   WEDGE 3.   ARMATURE ⓓ

Index